Liberal Education

Re-examined

Liberal Education

Re-examined

ITS ROLE IN A DEMOCRACY

by

A Committee appointed by the
American Council of Learned Societies

THEODORE M. GREENE
Chairman
CHARLES C. FRIES
HENRY M. WRISTON
WILLIAM DIGHTON
Secretary

HARPER & BROTHERS PUBLISHERS

NEW YORK AND LONDON

9999

Contents

FOREWORD BY WALDO G. LELAND   vii

PREFACE   ix
1. THE GENERAL NATURE OF THE REPORT
2. HOW THE REPORT WAS PREPARED
3. IMPORTANCE OF THE INQUIRY

CHAPTER I. EDUCATION IN AMERICA TODAY   1
1. THE CONTEMPORARY SCENE IN PERSPECTIVE
2. AMERICAN EDUCATION IN PERSPECTIVE
3. LIBERAL EDUCATION IN PERSPECTIVE

CHAPTER II. THE IDEAL OBJECTIVES OF A DEMOCRACY   21
1. DEMOCRACY AND THE IDEAL OF FREEDOM
2. THREE MAJOR PREMISES OF DEMOCRACY
    (a) SELF-GOVERNMENT IS POSSIBLE
    (b) ONLY DEMOCRACY IS CONSISTENT WITH MATURE HUMAN DIGNITY
    (c) A MAJOR FUNCTION OF GOVERNMENT IS TO PROTECT THE RIGHTS OF ITS CITIZENS

CHAPTER III. THE IDEAL OBJECTIVES OF EDUCATION IN A DEMOCRACY   31
1. THE AUTHORITARIAN AND DEMOCRATIC OBJECTIVES IN EDUCATION
2. EDUCATION FOR THE GOOD LIFE
    (a) THE GOOD LIFE DEFINED IN TERMS OF INTRINSIC VALUES
    (b) THE SCHOOL AS ONE AMONG MANY EDUCATIONAL AGENCIES
    (c) LIBERAL EDUCATION THE PRIMARY CONCERN OF THE SCHOOL
3. EDUCATION FOR CITIZENSHIP AND POLITICAL LEADERSHIP
4. TRAINING IN SPECIFIC VOCATIONS AND PROFESSIONS
5. THE GOOD LIFE, DEMOCRACY, AND LIBERAL EDUCATION

CHAPTER IV. THE CONTENT OF A LIBERAL EDUCATION 45

  1. MATHEMATICS
  2. THE NATURAL SCIENCES
  3. THE SOCIAL STUDIES
  4. THE HUMANITIES

    A. THE NATURE AND STUDY OF LANGUAGE
    B. THE ARTS AND LITERATURES
    C. MORALITY AND RELIGION
    D. THE CENTRAL ROLE OF THE HUMANITIES
  5. HISTORY AND PHILOSOPHY

CHAPTER V. EDUCATION AT THE VARIOUS ACADEMIC LEVELS 79
  PART I 79

    1. THE ELEMENTARY SCHOOL
    2. THE SECONDARY SCHOOL
    3. THE FOUR-YEAR COLLEGE
    4. THE PREPARATION OF TEACHERS
    5. THE GRADUATE SCHOOL

  PART II 100

    1. OBJECTIVES AND CONDITIONS OF LIBERAL EDUCATION
    2. THE ELEMENTARY SCHOOL
    3. HIGH SCHOOL AND PREPARATORY SCHOOL
    4. THE FOUR-YEAR COLLEGE COURSE
    5. VOCATIONAL AND PROFESSIONAL TRAINING

CHAPTER VI. CONCLUSION 115

BIBLIOGRAPHY 121

Foreword

THE American Council of Learned Societies, which, by the terms of its constitution, is devoted to "the advancement of the humanistic sciences," is of necessity concerned with the place of the humanities in education at all levels, and with the influence of educational trends upon the humanistic studies. It realizes its obligation to work constantly for the truly effective functioning of the humanities as an educational force.

Resolutions addressed to the Council by the American Philological Association, one of its constituent societies, inspired the organization of an important symposium in the Council's annual meeting of January, 1938, which was devoted to the consideration of the effects of twentieth century educational trends upon the place of the humanistic studies in school and college curricula. In this discussion there participated representatives of special committees of the Modern Language Association of America, of the National Federation of Modern Foreign Language Teachers, and of the Classical Association of the Middle West and South. An immediate result of the discussion was the preparation in the Executive Offices of the Council of a draft of a plan for a thorough-going study of the place of the humanities in education. Before undertaking this study, however, it was decided to refer the draft to a special committee, which was asked to advise the Council as to the most effective and appropriate way in which it might deal with the general problem, and especially as to what preliminary studies or explorations might be useful.

The committee thus appointed consisted of Professor Theodore Meyer Greene of Princeton University, chairman, President Henry M. Wriston of Brown University, Professor Charles C. Fries of the University of Michigan, and Mr. William Dighton of Queens College, secretary.

This committee was instructed that the chief concern of the

Council was not for the "defense of the humanities," but for the making of a positive and constructive effort to develop the full values of the contribution that the humanities must make to education and to life.

The committee, after consideration and with the approval of the Council's Executive Committee and Advisory Board, decided to interpret its mandate broadly, and, instead of merely advising the Council as to further action, to undertake a discussion of the nature of liberal education and of the place of the humanities therein.

Accordingly, the committee prepared a statement which has been widely discussed, within and without the Council, and which has undergone many revisions. In its present and final form the statement is offered to the general public as a contribution to the discussion of an educational problem that has assumed, in these days of war, a position of the utmost importance and urgency.

The statement is not, however, put forth as a statement *by* the American Council of Learned Societies. Such a body as the Council, of composite membership and of widely varying views, does not, if it is wise, pronounce collectively upon the problems which it takes under consideration. Indeed, it is most improbable that any large body of free scholars could reach unanimous agreement upon any collective announcement involving opinions and judgments of values.

This attitude on the part of the Council should not, however, affect the reception of the statement which its initiative has caused to be prepared by a small group of responsible and competent scholars. The value of the statement will be determined, as such values are always determined, by its intrinsic merit, by the response of the public to which it is addressed, and by its influence upon the situation with which it deals.

WALDO G. LELAND,
Director,
American Council of Learned Societies

Preface

〰〰

THE American Council of Learned Societies has for many years been promoting, with notable success, scholarly inquiries in the fields included under the "humanities." But it has become increasingly aware of various forces in American culture, and trends in American education, which threaten the very basis of all scholarship. It therefore appointed a committee, in 1940, to investigate recent educational trends in the humanities and to consider the causes responsible for them.

1. *The General Nature of the Report*

The committee has not conceived its task to be primarily fact-finding or statistical. There already exist innumerable studies of this type, and many of these we have scrutinized with care (see Bibliography). The committee has attempted, rather, to describe certain pervasive characteristics of American society and American education, and to formulate basic cultural ideals and educational objectives.

Nor has the committee attempted to prescribe detailed and specific remedies for present educational deficiencies. It is integral to the democratic spirit and to the very concept of liberal education that the concrete realization of common ideals and objectives be left to individual initiative, and that regimentation be scrupulously avoided. No two educational institutions are identical; each has its own history and tradition, its own personnel and clientele, its own distinctive problems. Each has its own corporate individuality, and this individuality must be respected and defended at all costs. We have therefore deliberately refrained from making specific proposals which, in the nature of the case, could not be equally applicable to all, or even to many, diverse educational institutions. Our concern has been to define a common cultural and educational goal, not to specify in detail the means whereby this goal may gradually be approached.

This self-imposed restriction in no way lessens the importance of the task here undertaken. However great our diversity, we still have a fundamental unity. We are a people with a great common heritage, common needs, common ideals. The very fact that this heritage is too often ignored, these needs misconstrued, and these ideals conceived of in a confused manner, makes it imperative that from time to time, and especially in periods of national crisis, our common goal and the basic conditions of its approximation be redefined. Only thus can we hope to act wisely and to co-operate effectively. It is hoped that this report may help to provide a basis for such co-operation and render more effective our corporate educational endeavors. It will accomplish its purpose if individuals and groups in educational institutions throughout the country will attempt, on their own initiative and responsibility, to actualize the ideals here envisaged.

It will be evident that the committee has not restricted itself to a consideration of the "humanities" in the narrower meaning of the term, that is, to the academic disciplines and modes of activity which that term commonly connotes. The true nature and value of the humanities can be understood only in a wider context, namely, in the context of a liberal education. Nor can the nature and value of liberal education be discussed effectively save in the still wider context of basic cultural and human ideals. These ideals, in turn, take on meaning only in a concrete social and political setting; our form of government and our democratic way of life are clearly essential to American culture and are relevant to our larger objectives.

The organization of the report reflects this wider perspective. In order to approach the problem of education in America in a realistic way we have asked ourselves two questions: (a) Where are we now? What is the present situation? (b) Where do we want to go? What are our ultimate objectives? We have discussed these two questions in turn, bearing in mind that our educational goal must be defined in its cultural setting and that any program for future activity must be formulated with regard both to the past and to the present.

More specifically, we have attempted, in the first chapter, to describe certain characteristics of American culture which have reflected themselves in American education. The next two chapters attempt a reformulation of the enduring objectives of American democracy and of the ideal goal toward which education in such a democracy should move. The nature of a liberal education is examined more closely in Chapters IV and V, with special regard to its essential subject matter and its potential effectiveness at the various academic levels. Here recognition is given to the unique importance of the "humanities" in the narrower sense.

2. How the Report Was Prepared

In order that the report may contribute to a nation-wide effort to revitalize liberal education, the committee has tried to ascertain representative opinion in various educational circles in different parts of the country.

First of all, the chairman of the committee spent eight weeks visiting a large number of representative colleges and universities in the East, South, Far West, and Middle West. He gave a talk in each of these institutions outlining some of the main ideas which the committee proposed to elaborate in the report, and then spent from one to three days discussing these ideas with administrative officers, faculty, and students. In these talks he discovered wide agreement on the chief needs and major objectives of liberal education; he also discovered how differently institutions were attempting to solve their educational problems.

On his return, the chairman wrote a first draft of the report. This draft was scrutinized by the other members of his committee and multigraphed copies of it, further revised, were widely circulated for more detailed criticisms. These were taken into account in a second draft, which was again widely circulated. Copies of this draft were sent to all the members of the Association of American Colleges and a full day of its annual meeting held in Pasadena was devoted to a discussion of the report led by the chairman. Careful analysis of all the sug-

gestions and criticisms of the second draft led to the omission of
the original two introductory chapters, and President Wriston
was asked to write the present Chapter I to take their place. The
present Chapters II and III were extensively revised. Chapter
IV, on the content of liberal education, remains with few altera-
tions. Because of the complexity of the problem of liberal education at the several academic levels, it seemed desirable to
discuss it from two complementary approaches. Chapter V is
accordingly divided into two parts. Part I, by Professor Fries,
discusses the problem in the light of present academic practices,
while Part II, by the chairman, states the case in the light of the
basic assumptions of the report.

When the report was presented to the American Council of
Learned Societies, first for a preliminary discussion and then for
final action, it became evident that the scholars constituting this
body were themselves in sharp disagreement on many crucial
issues, and that it was impossible to draft a statement of this
type to which all the members of the Council could subscribe
without qualification. Dr. Leland has reported in the Foreword the policy adopted by the Council.

As was natural, the members of the committee also have
differed at times, though they have found themselves in substantial agreement on the basic character, objectives, and value
of liberal education. Each of us, accordingly, holds himself
specifically responsible for what he has written—President
Wriston, for Chapter I; Professor Fries, for Part I of Chapter V;
Mr. Dighton, for the Appendix; and the chairman, for the re-
mainder of the report. But we endorse in general the report
as a whole, though each with certain qualifications regarding
the contributions of one or other of his colleagues.

The report is thus more than a symposium of individual
opinions. Our protracted committee discussions have resulted
in a large measure of agreement. That the report is not
unanimously approved in every detail by the entire committee,
and that each of us inevitably reflects his temperamental and
professional approach in what he has written, is inevitable and,
we believe, not unhealthy. In any case, we have followed
the only procedure which seemed to us honest and feasible.

I wish to thank all the members of my committee for their patient and willing co-operation. I am deeply indebted to Mr. Dighton for his assistance in the preparation of the report in its several drafts, and particularly for his collaboration on the chapters for which I, as chairman, must accept formal responsibility. The committee is also grateful to him for his analysis and tabulation of criticisms and for his efficient discharge of his many other secretarial duties.

I wish to thank Dr. David O. Robbins for his criticism of the first draft of Chapter IV.

3. Importance of the Inquiry

The importance of liberal education for American democracy can hardly be exaggerated. The war which is now being waged involves, at least in part, a conflict between two radically divergent philosophies. One of these is coercive and authoritarian; the other is persuasive and dedicated to liberty. The nations committed to the authoritarian ideal have discovered the importance of propaganda and its effectiveness in inculcating its ideal in the minds of the people and in achieving national unity. If democracy is to make headway against authoritarianism, it must rely on a form of education which is as effective for the promotion of democratic ideals and the liberal spirit as propaganda has been effective for the achievement of authoritarian ends. How is this to be done? Not by propaganda, regimentation and coercion, for these devices, if resorted to, would be self-defeating. We must rely rather on understanding and self-imposed discipline, on free and willing co-operative effort. But such understanding and co-operation can be achieved only if our common objectives are clearly defined and widely appreciated.

Democratic procedure is in very essence self-critical. The democratic spirit manifests itself in man's ability and willingness to subject himself to self-scrutiny. We offer no apology, therefore, for writing a report which is in many respects critical of prevalent administrative attitudes and educational practices. Nor do we consider it idle to hope that the report may receive the support of those who feel impelled to apply our critique to themselves. It is our thesis that American education, though healthy in many respects, is deficient in other respects, and that we can effect the necessary reforms only through self-examination and self-criticism.

Finally, it should be pointed out that the report deals not only with enduring objectives but also with the immediate situation and the present need for remedying our educational deficiencies. The ultimate goal of education is as enduring as human nature itself, and a judicious definition of this goal is as relevant in one age and culture as in another. But the concrete situation in which a society finds itself changes from year to year, and the devices for social reform which are effective in one period may not be equally effective in another. The task of social reform necessitates concern with *both* ends and means, since ends can be distinctly envisaged only in concrete situations and realized only through the discovery and use of effective means, and since human action, in the absence of clearly defined ends, must remain undirected and potentially harmful. The educational world today presents us with many examples of well-intentioned activity which is harmful to the cause of education because those who are engaged in it have not clearly and wisely defined their ultimate educational objectives or chosen appropriate means to achieve them. We have tried to delineate enduring objectives and, at the same time, to keep in mind the relevance of these objectives to American education in our American democracy in this period of crisis. It is our hope that this analysis of the ideal of education in a democracy will prove to have enduring value. But it is also our hope that it will serve as a liberal and democratic manifesto or creed—as a platform upon which democratically and liberally minded citizens throughout the country may now unite and move in greater harmony and efficiency toward our common goal.

T. M. G.

Princeton, N. J.
March 1, 1943

Liberal Education
Re-examined

Chapter 1. EDUCATION IN AMERICA TODAY

1. *The Contemporary Scene in Perspective*

Any discussion of the liberal arts should lay its primary emphasis upon perspective; to fail to do so would betray them. Yet for many years perspective has been difficult to achieve. The present war makes it still more difficult in one sense but easier in another.

The war makes perspective more difficult because the day's news is so tragically dramatic that it tends to swallow up one's sense of proportion. The tragedy is grim enough in itself, but the drama is heightened artificially by the moment-to-moment insistence of the radio, the immediate telephoned pictures, and the proximately released newsreels.

From another point of view the war makes achievement of perspective much easier. The nation was born in a fight for freedom—and so this war is described. Dramatic coincidence also heightens the effect. Immediately after the declaration of war we celebrated the sesquicentennial of the Bill of Rights. All who asserted that it held the essence of the present struggle thus recognized the continuity of fundamental ideas and issues. This recognition signalized a sharp change from a mood which would tolerate nothing but a "new deal," a "new order," a revolution, either Marxist or Fascist. The discontinuity of history had furnished the theme for so long that the current realization of its unbroken thread comes with something of a shock.

When one considers education in America today, the first question to answer is: American education from what point of view? Its scale is so vast that no snapshot is possible. Currents of opinion and action are so varied, so intricate, in some places so complementary and elsewhere so contradictory, that they seem to defy accurate observation.

Attempts at generalization are bound to be controlled not

merely by the available objective data but by the values most prized by the individual observer. To one whose mind is analytical and whose predilections are for harmony of design, regularity of pattern, or uniformity of action, the American educational scene seems completely chaotic. He is eager for a "plan," a "method," a "system," for "standardization," for equalization of opportunities and facilities, for organization.

To one whose mind revels in variety, who likes contrast and the interplay of diverse forces, the current situation appears as a manifestation of enormous vitality, of great forces producing immense power and often brilliant light. Far from objecting to diversity, he is distressed at the degree to which education has borrowed the concept of standardized interchangeable parts from industry. To such a mind, "15 units" as a measure of "preparation" for college, or "120 hours" as a measure for attaining a degree are evidences of unwise regimentation, indeed of a misconception of the inner nature of the whole process. He takes comfort, however, in the realization that the standardized elements are not real; within those falsely labeled packages the contents vary so greatly that the labels are confusing only to the hopelessly naïve.

Such a mind interprets American education not as an organization which can be plotted upon a chart, but as something living and growing. It is not entirely, or even predominantly, logical, since growth is not governed by logic alone; all growth is unique, even within the classifications of genus and species. It is never in perfect balance, and could not be put, much less kept, in perfect balance. It represents the constant battle between growth and decay—life and death in perpetual struggle. Its dominant characteristic is vitality, which is the best evidence of growth.

In the United States, particularly, differences rather than uniformity will be regarded by such a mind as natural. Because its extent is so vast, the conditions of life arising from climate, soil, racial stocks, and many other factors are bound to produce enormous and healthy variations. These are revealed in the tone of voice, in the accent of speech, in the very rhythm of life. They necessarily affect the educational process. Only a powerfully supported and ruthlessly executed "plan" could possibly overcome them.

Looking at this matter objectively, it is obvious that there is some validity in both points of view. Even growth is not wholly beyond control—the tree is pruned, fertilized, sprayed, and otherwise cared for, and may even be adapted by espalier methods to a form quite unlike its natural shape, and yet bear good fruit. Growth need not be without stimulation. Organization can leave room for vitality and freedom.

Historically, the variety of chaos (depending upon the observer's point of view) has been stimulated by local control of education. Until recently the federal government has done almost nothing in the field of education. Modest subsidies of general and special programs, statistics, and information constitute its traditional contributions. Even state governments have done relatively little, either by money or by regulation; and what has been done has differed in each of the forty-eight states. The major initiative and the principal control have been local or "private." When men fasten their eyes upon small nations, or upon nations with centralized governments or a different philosophy of political control, the inactivity of the federal government and the modest activity of the states appear as "neglect." But by men devoted to the American tradition of individualism, the lack of centralized control is described as "wisdom."

Nearly all observers would agree that American education for the last twenty-five years has been dominated by a critical spirit. The important word is "dominated," for there has never been an age when there were not active and vocal discontents. The names of Horace Mann, Henry Barnard, Francis Wayland, and Charles William Eliot—to enumerate only a few—have been associated with demands for "reform." Indeed, the urge to reform is a characteristic American trait. It was noted by every foreign commentator from de Tocqueville to Bryce. The notion that there was ever a period of calm and peace in the educational world is simply bad history.

Nonetheless, there have been surges of discontent, and in the last quarter century the demand for reform, or at least for change, has mounted to a tidal wave. That is not surprising. The industrial and the agricultural revolutions enormously increased the wealth of the world during the nineteenth century. The potentialities for the abolition of poverty seemed about to come to fruition in the twentieth. The peace movement, the quarantine of war, and international law had the active endorsement of statesmen; the two Hague Conferences dramatized the hope of "permanent" peace.

Then the cataclysm of the World War swallowed up both peace and prosperity. Men were butchered on a scale never before known; enough wealth was destroyed to have banished the specter of want from the world. While fighting continued, the collapse of men's hopes was postponed by the spiritual quality of their sacrifice; the world was buoyed up by the thought that it was a war to end war. Men believed it was the last great struggle on the pilgrimage toward peace. They trusted that when swords should again be beaten into plowshares, poverty could actually be conquered.

The war was won, but the peace was lost. That proved even more tragic than the war itself. With that failure man lost faith in his kinship to divinity and became obsessed with his own bestiality. Art and literature, education and religion, politics and business alike laid a heavy accent upon failure and frustration. Beauty in art was damned as pretty; stark "realism" turned to powerful ugliness, or went mad in surrealism, or precipitated escape into abstractionism. Serious music reveled in dissonance, popular music abandoned itself to jungle rhythms and the moaning frustrations of the "torch song." *Babbitt, An American Tragedy, Desire Under the Elms, Journey's End, Tobacco Road* set the dreary stage of realism in literature and the theater. The politicians smeared the businessman as a profiteer, and business blamed politics for its failures; both misapprehended spiritual weaknesses as mere economic or political dislocations. Deep underlying skepticism withered loyalties to all institutions alike—democratic, economic, and Christian. Anyone who insisted upon regarding history as a record of human progress was considered a fool. Unless a man stood and proclaimed, "Behold, I make all things new," he was denied a hearing.

This setting was perfect for the revolutionary spirit, which is as ruthless in destroying discredited institutions as it is vigorous in building new ones. Fascism was distressingly liberal with castor oil, but it cleaned up Italy, made trains run on time (both reforms especially appealing to Americans), and awakened a new spirit of hope and confidence in a jaded nation. There was even some grudging admiration for Hitler's restoration of German discipline and morale. The Russian revolution lost, after a time, the terror which was an incident of its destructive phase and acquired the substitute terror of success. Discontented people were impressed by "plans" which were transforming the society of Russia and its economy, while disheartened democrats became afraid of its political expansion through the process of infiltration.

The revolutionary emphasis upon the discontinuity of history, and the promise of a better pattern of life written upon fresh paper, seemed to many more appealing than further scribblings upon the palimpsest of experience, already confused by much superimposed writing. The illusion of a "new" world appeared in many forms in America, as elsewhere. Here its political manifestations were relatively mild in substance, despite verbal insistence upon historical discontinuity. But perspective was impaired by the habit of fixing attention upon change rather than continuity. The distortions occasioned by the emphasis on change were aggravated by neglect of all that had remained the same. The pace of change was speeded up by the simple device of failing to take cognizance of intermediate stages. Seldom was any period mentioned between the "horse and buggy" days and those of the airplane.

This sense of living in a new age, broken from the past by a kind of fatal discontinuity, gave the impression that the troubles of this age were unique. Therefore reasons without a high degree of validity were assigned for these troubles. Proposals for treatment were offered on the basis of superficial symptoms, whereas the groundwork of any clinical diagnosis is a careful review of the case history of the patient. The shallow assumption that all the problems of the age were new made men scorn the cumulative wisdom of human experience in solving current difficulties. They forgot that, beneath the veneer of present circumstances, most important problems are old, and that every vital issue has been wrestled with by previous generations. The Dust Bowl, for example, became the hysterical symbol of rich land destroyed by wrong treatment. The commonly accepted interpretation overlooked the available and revealing history of drought; when the rains came the diagnosis was washed out. The Joad family flashed across the social scene as utterly tragic but wholly typical. Dogmas of despair went unchallenged because of failure to examine the long, continuous record.

It was assumed that we live in a new world merely because of the miracles of speed in transportation and communication. They were held to have created a new world structure, a new interdependence. These assumptions neglected the simple fact that the colonial empires of Spain and Portugal were four hundred years old, and those of the Dutch and British over three hundred. The world colonial system existed long before the acceleration of speed of communication. It was forgotten that embattled farmers over a century and a half before had fired a "shot heard round the world"—not transmitted by the radio, it is true, but by waves just as sensitive. In short, the miracles of communication were not appraised accurately, and their effect was overestimated. They were important but not so decisive as was supposed.

Another factor held responsible for creating a "new" world was the machine. It was assumed that civilization had been wholly transformed by machines, and the inference was drawn that man himself had somehow been altered. Nothing is more amazing than the forms of idolatry which have shown themselves through the ages. It seems hardly credible that men would make a golden calf and then worship the product of their own workmanship; yet something of the same fear and awe appeared in the twentieth century attitude toward the machine. Those who created the machine felt that it in turn had created a new world.

The sense of discontinuity had also, quite irrationally, been heightened by mistaken inferences and analogies from science. The analytical method—counting, measuring, gathering data by the processes of research—was overplayed at the expense of both the historical approach and the systematic method of philosophy. All too often it was forgotten that "the elementary data of the American record should be independent of the mood of the moment."

2. American Education in Perspective

This tragic sense of discontinuity made its inevitable impact upon educational thought. Education had been a glowing faith throughout most American history. Suddenly, because it had not prevented war or depression or hardship, it was said to have "failed." Criticism of its institutions followed the dominant pattern of negativism, and a "new" education was the inevitable demand.

The liberal arts were the traditional heart of the "old" education; therefore, they must be abandoned. It was claimed that the characteristic studies were no longer relevant; they did not contribute directly or materially to the new social order. It was essential to substitute something new, which was given the vague name of "general" education, a spiritually neutral word, devoid of any implications of insight, perception, values.

The critics argued that the classics were merely dead languages from a bygone era which had imposed themselves upon youth through the sheer weight of tradition. They had been retained by colleges too conservative to recognize the new day. This argument totally overlooked the fact that the classics had never been "relevant," in any direct and immediate sense, to the ages in which they were studied. The world of the Renaissance was so different from the world of classical antiquity that, even then, not much of a case could be made for the "practical utility" of classical studies. These studies were real and vital during the Renaissance because classical literature was explored with tremendous energy, with freshness of vision, with enthusiasm, and with an earnest desire to cull from it beauty and wisdom. If the classics were studied today with like enthusiasm, with like energy, and with like determination to find in them the secrets of the greatness of ancient culture, they would possess for us a comparable value.

The criticism of the classics and other liberal studies wholly overlooked the fact that the traditional curriculum, even in its purest form, never guaranteed a liberal education. For example, the British universities in the early nineteenth century were based upon the liberal arts. Despite the fact that they were devoted to those studies, they lacked vitality and the product of their instruction was unsatisfactory. "A corrupt sleep . . . hung heavy over the English and Scottish centers of learning," and contemporaries declared there was no chance of "reform from within."[1] George Ticknor said at the end of the first quarter of the nineteenth century, "Who has been taught anything at our colleges with the thoroughness that will enable him to go safely and directly onward to distinction in the department he has . . . entered without returning to lay anew the foundations for his success?"[2]

Any belief in the validity of experience would instantly warn us that no body of subject matter, by itself, is liberal. The genius of man cannot be wrapped up in a neat curricular package. Only liberally minded teachers and students can achieve a liberal education; for such education depends essentially upon contact of mind with mind in dealing with significant ideas. Some studies have served vastly better than others as a medium for significant intellectual exchange. But the best tool makes a botched job in the hands of a careless or incompetent workman. On the other hand, a skilled, resourceful, and industrious craftsman can do a reasonable job with imperfect tools. This constitutes no argument for poor tools, but it is conclusive demonstration of the essential need for competent workmen.

Historically some disciplines may be regarded as much more mature than others. They have been the subjects of instruction literally for centuries. In the course of grappling with those problems again and again, the methods of attack have been refined,

[1] James B. Conant, "Academical Patronage and Superintendence," *Occasional Pamphlets of the Graduate School of Education,* Harvard University, No. 3 (June, 1938), pp. 1, 14.
[2] *Remarks on Changes Lately Proposed or Adopted in Harvard University* (Boston, 1825), p. 45.

fallacious techniques have been identified, ideas and insights have been reviewed, criticized, sharpened, and made more appealing and effective. That gives to these studies, which are the substance of the liberal arts, a unique quality which other disciplines can acquire only after like periods of developing maturity.

The theory that all materials of study should be directly "relevant" to current problems was never philosophically defensible. Practically it has broken down completely. After a quarter of a century of railing at mathematics beyond arithmetic as useless in a day of adding and calculating machines, of interest and rate tables, of gasoline pumps that show the cost as well as the amount of the sale, war has come. Now there is an urgent demand for all sorts of persons of whom we were said to have a "surplus" only five years ago. Engineers, physicists, fliers, deck officers, artillerymen, and hundreds of others must have the mathematics which was "needless" but yesterday. Of course the exponents of liberal education never defended mathematics on such transitory grounds alone, but on its inherent qualities. Mathematics was no more "useful" to a medieval monk or to a Renaissance painter, certainly no more apposite or appropriate, than it is to one who lives in a modern industrial society. But there always has been, and always will be, need for rigorous thinking, for thinking detached from self-interest. That is why mathematics has remained one of the fundamental disciplines. As one of the most precise and beautiful mental constructs of man it has its own intrinsic value, a value quite independent of considerations of utility.

Similarly, foreign languages were believed irrelevant in an isolated America, and their traditional grip upon schooling had to be broken. This point of view still prevailed when world-wide broadcasting was making foreign languages a daily diet of more people than ever before in history, and on the eve of a polyglot war in which Americans are fighting on five continents!

From the standpoint of a liberal education, however, much more was involved in slighting the foreign languages than the direct consequences of shallow concentration upon transitory environmental circumstances. More significant was the fact that students were deprived of an essential linguistic discipline without which their intellectual development was partial and lopsided. Moreover, they lost a precious opportunity, which no substitute discipline could supply, for participating directly and richly in the insights and expressions of some of the world's great minds. A needless barrier prevented them from acquiring a broad world view.

Many other illustrations could be cited to show that a short-run educational objective is self-defeating even from the "practical," but more essentially from the liberal, point of view, and that the whole doctrine of "relevance" is anti-educational in its effects. The belief that education should, above all else, make a direct impact upon contemporary problems leads to frequent reversals of position. Five or six years ago the group who insisted upon that point of view sought to use educational facilities as a kind of glorified youth hostel, a refuge from unemployment for millions of youth for whom industry would "never" find a need. The same group is now indignant that the schools and colleges hold youth too long into adult life and waste "precious" time needed for essential productive effort. After a frantic search for some years for teaching materials relevant to the dreaded "new leisure," educators are now making an equally frantic effort quickly to provide material relevant to the present crisis. The doctrine of relevance is valid only in a perfectly stable world where the future is easily predictable—obviously an impossible condition in a "new" world, or in an "old" one either.

Among the arguments for the so-called failure of liberal education was the assertion that it constituted an escapist retreat into an ivory tower. But the ivory tower argument will not stand analysis. It has a concealed major premise, hidden because it is absurd, that there are only two possible locations: either an ivory tower, remote from reality, or the market place, in the midst of the throng. It has a minor premise which is also concealed, namely, that man spends his entire life in the ivory tower and never in the market place or, *per contra*, always in the market place, never in the ivory tower. Both the major premise and the minor premise are incorrect.

One does not create an airplane solely in the factory amidst the hum of machines and in a welter of materials. The distinctive idea for its design may have been a happy inspiration on a remote mountain peak. Long before it is translated into materials, there is an infinitude of calculation, some of it of the most abstruse kind; there are hundreds of blueprints, many of them extraordinarily detailed in character. Part of the operation takes place in the ivory tower, part in the market place.

If there were no ideas except those which men have on the production line, or if, on the contrary, the ideas men have on the mountaintop were never translated into actuality, this would be a different world. Not only are both sorts of experience valid, but so also are many experiences which are intermediary—which lie between the two extremes, and which neither figure of speech aptly characterizes. The home, for example, is neither an ivory tower nor a market place.

The application of this discussion to the problem of education is obvious. If the schools are concerned solely with the market place, they are the creatures of their environment; they are merely reflections of the bustling activity which there takes place; they are primarily concerned with the vocational aspects of life; they are kaleidoscopic mirrors of society and not instruments for its development or control; they may well be as confused as the traffic at the busy mart.

Men of action need occasionally to withdraw to some quiet place to reflect. Religion is remote from reality only when it is decadent; it is commercial only when it is corrupt. It has always been true in history that, though the church was near the center of activity, it did not perform its true functions when it was turned into a place of exchange and became itself the market. So it is with the school.

On the other hand, the high ideals, the noble thoughts, the righteous habits would be preserved only in a small group, and would not become a vital element in the general culture, if it were possible, as rarely in history it has been possible, to withdraw completely from the life of the world. Looking back over the history of American education, the imputation of withdrawal to an ivory tower does not apply to the colleges of liberal arts. They have richly fertilized American life and thought.

The plain truth is that cultural value means much more than immediate contemporary relevance and that accent on practical relevance has too often masked a retreat from the ideal of genuine education. This emphasis represented one phase of an over-dependence upon specific training. The essential difference between education and training is simple but basic. "Education" is designed to prepare men to do what they have never done before. Its emphasis is upon power to adapt oneself and go on alone. "Training" seeks to supply the skills and techniques to do again and again what has once been learned. Training is essentially a static concept, as education is dynamic. "Relevance" was the new "training" substitute for the old "educational" discipline. It is true that the formal discipline of the classical curriculum had, in course of time, become a mockery. But with its destruction, and the abuse of its cadaver long after its life was spent, all mental discipline became suspect. The discipline of conduct was interpreted as a form of the old tyranny which should have no place in the new freedom. The new ideal belittled the discipline of the home as well, and the discipline of tradition. All these had "failed." Thus allegiance to the notion of discontinuity precluded any profound appreciation of culture as a continuing phenomenon. It is not too much to say that culture always sells at a heavy discount in a "new" world, whether the frontier is physical or ideological.

The liberal quality of education was bound to suffer by having the darling of the new education dominate what was left of the old. Science was too triumphant to be denounced. It was assumed, therefore, that if the methods of science could be applied to older subjects, they might acquire its merits. Educational innovations furnish the perfect example. Measures, statistics, "research," "matched experiments," and a dozen other importations transformed pedagogy into pseudo-scientific education. Occasionally pedagogical contortions almost passed the boundaries of belief. In one specific instance, life activities were analyzed into ten categories—social intercommunication, physical power, practical labor, vocation, citizenship, social relationships, leisure activities, mental efficiency, religious activity, and home duties. Further analysis revealed that there were eleven hundred and seventeen separate abilities necessary to perform those activities—not eleven hundred and sixteen or eleven hundred and eighteen. Scientific work is always precise!

Under the same "scientific" impulse, literature was dissected and picked to pieces like a beetle in a laboratory. The social sciences lost their humanity in a false scientism that tended to make them sterile. After years of substituting information for wisdom, the Regents Inquiry finally made the amazing but obvious discovery that possession of facts supplies neither the incentive nor the direction for their proper use. Facts and values belong in different realms. It would be amusing, if it were not tragic, to realize that a period which laid so much emphasis upon relevance of materials laid so little upon relevance of method in studying those materials. It has long been clear that science has a great part to play in liberal education. But it should be equally clear that it must play its role directly, not by imposing its characteristics upon other disciplines whose methods and results, equally valid, are simply different.

Obsession with a sense of failure had extraordinary consequences. A generation newly aware of psychology and psychiatry was almost morbid in its fear of the word "fear." Many school systems went so far as to abolish the grade of failure, as though refusal to recognize a common and inevitable experience would banish it from the realm of reality. Others sought to mitigate its devastating effect with the slogan: "the failure of the student is the failure of the teacher"; thus the psychological damage was transferred from resilient youth to the harried adult. Still others sought to explain this distressing and all too common human trait by insisting that it was not laziness or other personal qualities which produced failure, but "inappropriate" materials. It was broadly intimated that any normal mind would revolt from the traditional subjects and would therefore naturally "fail" when confronted with such a diet of dust and ashes. For example, a pamphlet on "What the High Schools Ought to Teach," published by the American Council on Education, said: "Most secondary schools include in the ninth grade a course in algebra and in the tenth grade a course in demonstrative geometry, which, for want of alternatives, become required courses for most pupils. These two courses are recognized as stumbling blocks for many pupils. The failures in both of them are so high that they discourage no small number of young people from continuing in school."

Failure thus became in this new and topsy-turvy world an institutional, not a personal, matter. Any timidity in using the word to describe the shortcomings of individuals disappeared when an institution or when society at large was under discussion. The pamphlet just quoted had one section devoted to "Vicious aspects of the ninth grade." The very title is an assault upon the integrity or the intelligence of those regarded as responsible.

This accent on failure laid an extraordinary burden upon education, for it induced a common assumption that reform is impossible unless and until complete failure is admitted. Thus anyone who spoke of the great achievements of the past was instantly identified as one who sought to resist change. It was no accident that the period was marked by a "realistic" re-evaluation of American heroes. They belonged to a past which had failed. Their weaknesses and shortcomings were accented, and the debunking process was often carried to absurd extremes. Anyone who discussed the beneficial and successful aspects of education was damned as a conservative, the word acquiring the qualities of an epithet. He was considered a reactionary opponent of what was new and therefore better, for in a period which believed in discontinuity, any attempt to make the dead past live again was regarded as a hostile act. Often the situation approached the borderline of farce, so that only those who were ready to assert that all the toil and energy, all the sacrifice and skill, all the character and brains poured into the cultural and educational enterprise had resulted in failure were really progressive and ready for new developments.

Historically the precise reverse is true. Reform has proceeded best by capitalizing upon the momentum of success for further progress. If monumental efforts have been nugatory, there is little heart or energy for new projects of reform. Of course, desperate situations arise, when revolution is the only hope, but if one looks back over the history of the world, he must admit that more progress has been made by evolution than by revolution. The triumphs of manufacture—as in the automobile—are based upon refining and improving earlier successes. The great achievements of science have been made by capitalizing success, building fresh achievements upon old conquests.

So also, if we study the matter calmly, we find that the greatest successes of education have consisted in advances from strong positions. Take one outstanding achievement, desperately discounted during the recent pessimism—higher education for women. It was founded upon the success of men's colleges. Starting slowly, then gathering momentum, it overcame opposition. The triumph has become so complete that we now tend to discount it and to forget how much boldness, how much imagination, how much wisdom were required to launch it and to surmount obstacles. In like manner, recent critics have underestimated the really great progress in the democratization of education. Carping utopians insisted that American education is a failure because it is not equally open to all classes of people. They quote the phrase from the Declaration of Independence about being born equal, as though it were already a completed achievement in 1776, rather than a bold prophecy. Our progress toward that goal of perfect equality is belittled by comparing our current status with a remote ideal—leaving out of account the realities of the world in which we live and the genuine progress which has been achieved.

America has certainly led in the democratization of education, in making it available to people of lesser means. It is well known that not only do large numbers, but a much larger percentage of our youth go on to institutions of higher education today than ever before. The plain fact, which should be admitted by the most critical commentator, is that education at all levels, from highest to lowest, instead of being limited as time passes to persons of larger and larger incomes, has progressively been made available to students of relatively lower and lower economic status. The whole development of American higher education, the establishment of junior colleges, of state universities, of land-grant colleges, illustrates this trend. And anyone having the slightest familiarity with the capstone of American education—graduate study—recognizes that those who receive the longest and most costly training are not the wealthy or those most able to pay. Quite the reverse. The subsidy to graduate students is great. The field of graduate work is dominated by an aristocracy of interest and capacity, not by a group characterized by economic privilege.

Such a statement does not, of course, intimate that we have reached the desirable goal outlined by Jefferson well over a century ago of opening the path to learning to all men of capacity without any reference whatever to their economic status. That any competent man should be inhibited in his educational development by lack of financial resources constitutes not only a social but an intellectual tragedy. While, therefore, we can take comfort in the enormous progress already made, there is every reason to press forward toward the attainment of the ideal.

Within the limits of achievements in that direction, however, this much can be said. If one were to search for a modern illustration of the classless society, he would find it more nearly exemplified in the educational world than anywhere else. Teachers are drawn from every economic level, every social background. Students in like manner represent extraordinary differentiation in respect to ability and economic resources and cultural heritage. They are diverse in every way in which human beings can be diverse, for the democratic classless society is in no way hostile to the idea of individualism; indeed it is essentially dependent upon individualism.

American colleges thus constitute a society within which a person of vision and energy, industry and character, can go far toward making of himself what he wishes. They are places where one finds no educational privilege or right that is not bound up with an equivalent duty or responsibility. It is the essence of education that there is no special privilege which money can buy.

There is no educational distinction which birth can achieve. There is no attainment which a student can demand of his own right without having to win it. Participation in many extracurricular activities and in most honors awards, in Phi Beta Kappa and Sigma Xi, all depend upon ability and hard work. Rewards are not conditioned by anything but achievement, save in the rare instances where abuses have prostituted the normal functioning of the educational process. Even then the student can have only the husk of the reward without its substance.

Another great triumph of education which has sold at an unwarranted discount during this negative period is the advance in the quality, as well as in the range and inclusiveness, of its work. Two opposing factions here meet on common ground. One group, which regards itself as the exponent of reform, insists that standards have been kept so high that they discourage students. These people have dogmatically asserted that education is undemocratic because it is not geared to the intelligence of every citizen and therefore excludes from its presumed benefits those who are not able or willing to undergo the somewhat esoteric disciplines which traditionalists have fastened upon the schools.

The terrifying thing in the publications of these advocates of reform, so-called, is not the indictment they make of the educational process; it is the revelation of their lack of faith in the dignity, industry, and capacity of young people. It is a tragedy when youth falls into the hands of leaders who pity them instead of respecting them. This is the group which has sought to make young people sorry for themselves. As one of its leaders has said: "Thousands of young men and women leaving our schools each year are destined never to become self-supporting and independent in the sense that your and my generation was led to believe was our due. The supply of workers exceeds the demand. Man power is a drug on the market. The productive forces of this country are glutted with brain and brawn which they cannot use. And what can't be utilized is simply laid aside to moulder and decay."[3]

[3] Aubrey Williams before the National Council of Social Agencies in 1936, quoted in Lawrence Sullivan, *The Dead Hand of Bureaucracy* (New York, 1940), p. 254.

Though they talk of the "community centered school," these educators also taught youth to think less of others and more of themselves. They have made young people believe that they are underprivileged if they have to work hard. In an effort to prevent the exploitation of child labor, laws were passed and administrative regulations adopted which sometimes overshot their marks and effectively barred the way to giving youth economic experience. Some youth are obviously underprotected, but any objective review of the situation will offer convincing evidence that others have been overprotected. The consequences of this overprotection now lead to the denunciation of the schools because they are devoted only to intellectual tasks, rather than "useful work."

On the other hand, the self-styled educational reformers are met on common ground by academic hardshells who cry that standards have been lowered. The use of the word "standards" itself is revealing. It is borrowed from industrial practice and intimates measures which are definite and rigid, though no such measures exist or can exist in an enterprise like education. It predicates something absolute which is correct; everything else falls short. In human achievement that is a false, and even pernicious, assumption. It totally overlooks the nature of man and the historical realities of his experience.

It is to be hoped that higher education will escape from measuring intellectual achievement by the number of times a class meets in the course of a week, or by the number of semester hours taken. Attention should be concentrated not upon these falsely objective standards, but upon those norms which, though not mechanical, are no less real, and grow out of a consensus of informed opinion.

Numerous colleges of one hundred years ago would not be considered equal to many modern high schools. In the preparation of teachers, both in knowledge of their fields of instruction and in pedagogical skill, there has been an enormous advance. There have been some losses occasioned by overdependence upon "education" courses, and by registrar's arithmetic. But, broadly speaking, the talk of lowered standards stems from a false and deceptive terminology, from lack of historical perspective, from current pessimism about the present and alarm about the future, rather than from any just estimate of the actual situation.

Obviously, also, the quality of scholarship has improved in many respects in the last century. We have overcome many weaknesses. This is apparent when we remember the just criticisms of education one hundred years ago—of its overdependence on memory and its lack of emphasis on originality and creative work. Those were gross shortcomings. This is by no means to assert that present practice is beyond criticism or that it represents the ultimate in achievement. Admittedly there have been losses as well as gains; the "scientific" approach to liberal studies has sacrificed some of their humanistic qualities. The vital point to remember, however, is that emphasis on failure is not the best basis for reform. Further advance is best stimulated by realization of the successes already achieved. We can improve our work by setting our goals still further ahead, and by approaching them positively rather than by depreciating the substantial achievements of the recent past.

3. Liberal Education in Perspective

We have emerged from the period between two wars. Once again we are reminded that the great problems of mankind— peace, the pressure of population, health and prosperity, both physical and spiritual—are perpetual. They have a timeless quality. Very little written about "practical" matters even a few years ago is useful today; an account of a gas engine thirty years old would not serve our current needs. With ideas the picture is different. Plato and Aristotle are long dead, but they are still worth reading. The teachings of Jesus are very old, as we count time, yet in their essential qualities they are as fresh as yesterday. Changes in the economic structure, changes in the political order, changes in our environment—none of these impairs the wisdom which is the fruit of an intelligent mind activated by a warm heart. Liberal education seeks to bring into life greater refinement and greater intensity—to make it more sensitive, to make it more alive.

Viewed in this light, liberal education finds its full justification in its promotion of an intrinsically valuable experience. It is "preparation" for life only in the sense that its vital influence is continuous and leads ever on from one experience to others which are even richer. It finds its complete validation in every instance of physical, intellectual, emotional, and spiritual living upon an urbane and significant level. No boundaries of time inhibit it, and it is profoundly relevant to human life under all circumstances.

The war has precipitated a reassessment of values. The American people find themselves fighting to retain something precious. They recognize that things they took for granted, being now endangered, have greater values than those of which calloused familiarity had been aware. For years the accent has been on the failure of our institutions; now it is suddenly realized that with all their shortcomings, they are the most powerful and the most resilient in the world. Disastrous negative attitudes arose in a generation which had missed great prizes—peace and the conquest of poverty—by narrow margins, and having lost them, lost hope. Ortega y Gasset well described this epoch when he said that it was "superior to other times, [but] inferior to itself"; "strong, indeed, and at the same time uncertain of its destiny; proud of its strength and at the same time fearing it."

From the doubts and fears of that period the war launches us upon a fresh adventure. As the reassessment of values has reversed our trend in foreign policy, so also it may reverse other trends which have heretofore seemed too powerful to stem. The accent has switched from comfort and convenience to sterner virtues and more enduring values. Historically it has been under those conditions that the liberal arts are appreciated.

Chapter 2. THE IDEAL OBJECTIVES OF A DEMOCRACY

THE previous chapter attempted to sketch in broad outline some of the characteristics of American culture and the ways in which they have been reflected in American education. This account has brought to light certain deficiencies, both cultural and educational. But American democracy and American education both possess genuine vitality and express a way of life and a set of human ideals worthy of our loyalty. Our purpose in this and the following chapter is to attempt a restatement of these ideal objectives of democracy and education. Such a restatement should facilitate the effort to diagnose and assess the present educational scene and to suggest certain remedial principles where improvements are called for.

The assumption underlying this attempt is that ideals, clearly envisaged and consciously striven after, can operate as effective forces in a society. Both in our private lives and in our corporate activities we are, of course, profoundly influenced by geographic, economic, and other forces, and these forces unconsciously determine some of our objectives. But the more we are able to reflect, to consider alternative goals, to select those which most deeply satisfy our essential nature, and, in addition, to acquire an understanding of the various forces which impinge upon us, the better are we able to control these forces rather than be controlled by them. Though it must be admitted that all social institutions, including the school, do inevitably reflect the cultural pattern of any given period, it is equally true that such institutions can themselves, if they are vital, powerfully influence social ideals and social behavior. This is notably true of educational institutions. Their actual influence in our community is great, and their potential influence is enormous. The value of their contribution depends upon the wisdom and enthusiasm of their faculties, administrations, and governing bodies, that is, of the individuals in charge of the educational process. If they conform passively and uncritically to social trends, their institutions will indeed merely reflect current opinion and prevailing social and educational dogmas; if they are able to envisage an ideal goal, and if they can learn how to express their loyalty to this ideal, they can exert a powerful directive influence for good upon the community and the nation.

That educational institutions can assume this role is not a pious hope or a vague conjecture. Our own history, to say nothing of the history of Western culture, illustrates the compelling power of ideals, their origin in the minds of the more imaginative and articulate members of the community, and the role of the school in disseminating them. Recent events in Germany, for example, have shown how much educational institutions can do to influence public opinion. We in this country can compete with anti-democratic propaganda and instill in our young people, through liberal education instead of propaganda, loyalty to democratic ideals if we believe in them firmly and teach them effectively. Many of us today teach without basic conviction; we do not really believe in the importance of liberal education for life in a democracy. Hence our comparative ineffectualness. If we can capture a vision of our true objectives, and co-operate in steadfast loyalty to these objectives, we can be sure that our influence, as teachers and scholars, will be great.

1. Democracy and the Ideal of Freedom

Loss of faith in basic democratic principles can express itself in two ways which at first glance appear to lead in opposite directions but which in actuality tend to produce the same result. There is, on the one hand, the temptation to abandon the democratic form of government in favor of some form of dictatorship and, on the other hand, the tendency to make a fetish of democracy, to lose sight of the ultimate individual and social ends which democracy is designed to further. The latter tendency, were it to gain momentum, would also result, though in a more subtle and roundabout way, in the destruction of the democratic way of life, the stifling of the democratic spirit, and finally, the decay of democracy itself.

Men are tempted to abandon a democratic form of government whenever the pressure of events seems to necessitate more prompt and forceful social action than can easily be achieved by democratic methods. In periods of crisis it may indeed be necessary to curtail temporarily some democratic procedures, and to invest executive officers with unusual powers. But even such emergency measures need not, and should not, constitute an abandonment of the basic democratic principle that ultimate power and responsibility reside in the people and flow from the people to those in governmental authority. Loyalty to this principle is essential to the preservation of the democratic way of life and the democratic spirit.

Men tend to make a fetish of democracy when they forget that democracy is only a means, though an all-important means, to ultimate social and cultural ends. Especially at a time like the present, when emotions run high, when attention is focused on emergency measures to secure quick results, the impulse is strong to insist on superficial manifestations of patriotism and to lose sight of basic issues and vital stakes. The stronger this tendency, the greater the need for a clear understanding of the essential principles of democracy and the ends which it is its function to promote.

What, then, are the basic human ends which democracy should serve and from which democratic principles derive their value? They can best be described in terms of our traditional concept of freedom—freedom in the negative sense, as escape from harmful coercion, but also, and essentially, freedom in the positive sense, as the ability to live a rich and satisfying life. Positive and negative freedom imply each other, since man can hope to achieve the good life only in the absence of harmful coercions, and since coercions are harmful only when they inhibit the pursuit of positive goods. Freedom as absence of restraint, and freedom as the possibility of positive achievement, are thus two sides of the same shield. If their close interdependence is not forgotten, the distinction will help us to do greater justice to the full implications of freedom in its political, as well as its cultural, aspects.

The first great function of democracy is to safeguard man's

freedom in the negative sense, that is, to set up a political safe-guard against tyranny. History has shown that it is possible for an absolute monarch to be both wise and beneficent. But history also reveals the rarity of such rulers and the extreme unlikelihood of their being succeeded by rulers equally wise and beneficent. Where political power has been concentrated in the hands of a single individual, or of a small self-perpetuating group, it has sooner or later resulted in political tyranny, which, in turn, has usually led to economic, social, and religious oppression. One reason that democracy was prized so highly by the many genera-tions of men who fought to establish it on both sides of the Atlantic was that they conceived of it as the only possible pro-tection against tyranny and oppression. So long as ultimate political power rests in the hands of the people they can defend themselves, without recourse to violence or revolution, against exploitation by individuals and groups. Once they lose political control they are at the mercy of those into whose hands political power has fallen. This negative function of democracy is and must remain one of its essential justifications.

Yet it is clearly not enough that man should merely be freed from tyranny or harmful coercion. The good life has also a positive content; it is human existence rich in meaning, in happiness, in social and cultural achievement. What citizens crave is not merely freedom from unjustifiable restraint. They also crave the opportunity to explore and participate in all those experiences which have been found to yield intrinsic and lasting satisfaction. The democratic way of life is dedicated to the en-largement and deepening of the human spirit, both individually and collectively. It is a way of life in which the positive content of experience is of major importance. If it is to function as it should, democracy must therefore do everything that is appropri-ate and needful to enable its citizens to share, to the limit of their capacities, in this way of life.

2. *Three Major Premises of Democracy*

The democratic ideal rests on three premises. All three are explicitly challenged by the authoritarian ideal.

(a) *Self-government is possible.* The first is that the citizens in a democratic state are able to assume ultimate responsibility for their corporate life, that the men and women who enjoy the franchise have the capacity for responsible citizenship. What kind of ability is here assumed? To perform his duties as a citizen a voter must possess at least three qualifications.

He must, in the first place, be socially minded. That is, he must realize that he is a member of a social group and must have a genuine concern for the welfare of this group. He must be able to recognize the rights of other individuals, and he must understand that there are many things which both he and they prize which can be attained only through social co-operation. He must also realize that he is simultaneously a member of several social groups, some of which are small and closely knit, some more extensive and less tightly organized. The oldest and most cohesive group is the family, and it is in the family that social-mindedness is normally first acquired. Most individuals, as they grow up, join one or more organizations, fraternal, industrial, academic, and the like. Membership in these organizations also offers opportunity for the acquisition of social-mindedness. Men are also members of various political groups, local, state, and federal, and the nation to which they belong is one among many nations. A citizen should be aware of his affiliations with all these interlocking political groups; his social-mindedness should extend itself, so far as possible, from the town, county, and state to the nation and, finally, from the nation to the world. In his political thinking he should adopt not only a local and national but also an international perspective.

The second qualification for effective citizenship is an ability to grasp, at least in some measure, the import of basic issues, to distinguish between ends and means, and to evaluate alternative ends and alternative means for the achievement of these ends.

The third qualification is the ability to select political leaders with wisdom, and the willingness to respect their leadership. This is particularly important in a republican form of government in which so much authority is delegated to representatives.

These three qualifications are, of course, never completely

satisfied in any actual democracy. In no human society, however advanced, are all the citizens ideally social-minded, perfectly wise in their estimate of basic issues, infallible in their choice of leaders, or wholly judicious in their attitude toward those whom they have elected to office. This ideal can, however, be approximated in certain societies. The fact that democratic nations have endured through periods of crisis, and have manifested a notable degree of social cohesion and political wisdom, demonstrates the ability of the average voter to satisfy these conditions sufficiently to enable the democratic form of government to function with reasonable success. Events have proved that a majority of an electorate can manifest some measure of social-mindedness, some grasp of basic issues, and some discernment of, and respect for, political leadership. History does not justify an attitude of complete disillusionment and despair concerning the ability of the people to govern.

An authoritarian government rests on the opposite premise, that the common man is incapable of self-government and that it is impossible to equip him for political responsibility. A dictator asserts that he and his subordinates alone possess political wisdom, that it is their right and duty to assume absolute control of the body politic, and that every challenge of their self-proclaimed right to absolute power must be ruthlessly suppressed. This is one of the basic issues over which the present war is being fought.

(b) *Only democracy is consistent with mature human dignity.* The second premise of political democracy is that it is the only form of government consistent with human maturity and dignity, that is, that members of a politically mature society not only can but should assume ultimate political responsibility and keep ultimate power in their own hands. In an advanced society, so runs the democratic argument, the average citizen can acquire sufficient wisdom and a sufficient sense of responsibility to enable him to take an active part in government. Where this is possible, it is the citizen's moral duty to do so, because the democratic form of government is the only form of government which recognizes the right of mature individuals to determine their own destiny and which provides them with an opportunity to express themselves on political questions. This is the deep-seated conviction which is being emphasized today by the leaders of our democracies. Dictatorship enslaves men; democracy fosters human freedom. Only in a democracy is there a full recognition of human dignity and freedom, and of the rights of moral maturity.[1]

The moral justification for democracy is therefore not merely the defense which it alone provides against political and other coercions destructive of human dignity, but also, and more importantly, the outlet which it affords for positive moral action in the political realm. Moral maturity implies the right and the obligation to act as a free agent, both in private life and in corporate social activity. Political democracy is the only form of government which gives due recognition to this right and obligation. Democracy is therefore the ideal form of government in a society in which the majority of the voting citizens are sufficiently mature, morally and politically, to assume such responsibility.

Loyalty to the democratic principle does not involve dogmatic commitment to some specific form of organization. The basic democratic objectives can be achieved, or approximated, in different ways, and it is reasonable to assume that different social groups will, and should, employ different procedures. Any given society must work out its salvation in terms of its own particular history, temperament, and political genius. Nor need it be assumed that democracy is the only form of government in which individuals can live a rich and satisfying life. The good life is possible to *some* individuals in every form of society and under many different forms of government. The true democrat merely insists that democracy provides more people with a better opportunity to lead the good life than does any other form of government.

Finally, it is obvious that some societies are incapable of democracy, that democracy is a form of organization and control which some societies are not mature enough to achieve. The best that they can hope for is some form of paternalistic and benevolent autocracy. This fact, however, in no way invalidates the demo-

[1] This does not, of course, imply that culturally and spiritually mature *individuals* cannot live in an undemocratic state. We are concerned here only with the political implications of a mature *society*.

cratic ideal; it merely demonstrates the difficulty of approximating the ideal and indicates the conditions which must be satisfied if progress is to be made toward its realization.

(c) *A major function of government is to protect the rights of its citizens.* The third premise of democracy is that the duty of the state, as embodied in government, is to create the conditions under which each citizen can pursue happiness in his own way, provided only that his conduct does not jeopardize the equal right of others to lead their own lives. It is assumed, on the one hand, that government should control the lives and activities of its citizens as much as may be needful for the common welfare of all citizens. It is assumed also that the government is bound to protect its citizens from exploitation by any individuals or groups within the state.

Here again the authoritarian and democratic ideals are sharply at variance. The authoritarian theory of the state, denying that the individual as such is valuable, assumes that government should direct the lives of its citizens not only in the political domain but in the fields of morals and religion, artistic creation and intellectual inquiry, business and industry. The totalitarian ideal is the authoritarian ideal in one of its extreme forms, and "totalitarian" means total and complete control of the life of every man, woman, and child in the state. The democratic point of view, in contrast, assumes that it is the function of the citizens to control the government and to secure for each citizen the maximum freedom to lead his own life in his own way. The only proviso is that one citizen shall not exercise his freedom in such a way as to restrict the freedom of other citizens, and that one group shall not be permitted to tyrannize over another group. It is the function of those who are entrusted with governmental authority to ensure social welfare by defending, so far as possible, the right of each individual to select his own aims, and to achieve them as he sees fit.

Implicit in these three premises is the obligation of the state to see that provision is made for the education of its citizens. It is clear that the citizens of a democracy should be as well equipped as possible to engage in two distinguishable types of activity. They must be prepared, on the one hand, to exercise the franchise and, on the other, to lead their own lives as private individuals. Both types of activity, to be successful, require appropriate education, and it is essential that adequate opportunity for such education be made widely available. All citizens who expect to enjoy the franchise should be educated as effectively as possible for its intelligent use. Since the chief objective of a democratic state is to enable its citizens to participate in the good life as richly as their native endowments will permit, it becomes axiomatic that every citizen be educated to conduct his private life in a satisfying and socially beneficial manner.

These considerations, however, raise two important questions. How can our citizens best be educated for their political responsibilities and for life in a democratic community? And what specific responsibility should government assume for this education?

Our answer to the first question—an answer which will be developed in the following chapters—is that the most effective type of preparation both for citizenship and for the good life is a liberal education. Such education is, as we shall see, essentially cultural in content and reflective in approach. Its function is to introduce the student to his cultural heritage as adequately as his native ability and degree of maturity permit. It is also its function to discipline and guide him, during his formative years, to think clearly, evaluate wisely, and adopt a mature and responsible attitude. So conceived, a liberal education is informative—the student is introduced to facts with which he should be acquainted. It is disciplinary—the student is helped to acquire those habits of mind and instruments of investigation which he will need as he proceeds with his education. It is liberative—it gives him freedom of choice by making him aware of alternatives and thus widening the scope of his beliefs and actions. It is moral in the larger sense—the student is encouraged and helped to learn to think for himself and to approach intellectual and practical problems in a responsible manner. This is precisely the education requisite for responsible citizenship, and, simultaneously, the only effective education for the good life of the individual.

A judicious answer to the second question must take account

of the three premises just considered. The democratic emphasis on private initiative is certainly relevant to the field of education. The magnificent contribution to education which endowed institutions of all types have made in this country during the last three hundred years is a clear indication of how much can be accomplished in a free society by private initiative. Such institutions will have a continuing and indeed growing value in the future, for in them educational experiments can be conducted which would be difficult, if not impossible, in tax-supported institutions. On the other hand, private institutions have in the past not been able to provide adequate educational facilities for the entire population, and it is this deficiency which a democratic government must correct. This has been the motive and the justification for the establishment of public schools and tax-supported colleges and universities. The continuing need for such tax-supported institutions is apparent. Thus, both types of institutions have a distinctive contribution to make to American education, and each type can benefit from more effective co-operation with the other.

The ideal objective of our American democracy may therefore be summarized as the preservation and enhancement of human dignity and all that this implies—freedom from tyranny, opportunity for development and growth, enrichment of life, moral and spiritual maturity. To us the individual is of supreme import, and by an individual we mean a person able and willing to assume the ultimate responsibility for his private and social activities. The function of the state is to do everything in its power to foster human individuality, to encourage the truly liberal attitude, to enable its citizens to become "worthy of having been born free." The function of liberal education is to make men free and to teach them to bear freedom when they have it. In the words of Milton, "a complete and generous education is one that fits a man to perform, skillfully, justly, and magnanimously, all the acts, both public and private, of peace and war."

Chapter 3. THE IDEAL OBJECTIVES OF EDUCATION IN A DEMOCRACY

1. *The Authoritarian and Democratic Objectives in Education*

In an authoritarian state the individual belongs to the state and must make every sacrifice required of him by the state; man exists for the state, not the state for the welfare of the individual. Hence governmental control is emphasized at the expense of individual liberty; loyalty to the state is made a principal virtue; and the inculcation of such loyalty becomes the chief function of education. The good life is defined in terms of the potential contribution of each individual citizen to the state, and education for the good life is identified with training for membership in a totalitarian society. Education thus ceases to have the character which it ideally possesses in a free society and takes on the character of propaganda, that is, the indoctrination of the ideology approved by the state and conceived to foster the welfare of the state as a whole. The accent is on belief rather than on critical inquiry, on acquiescence rather than on reflection. Similarly, training for vocations and professions is designed to satisfy the needs of the corporate state. Men and women are trained for those vocations and professions which can contribute most to the political and social objective. In ultimate theory, the individual has no choice at all; his course is determined entirely by the requirements of functional efficiency.

In a democratic society, in contrast, the welfare of the individual as an individual is assigned supreme importance. Education designed to enrich the life and to foster the dignity of the individual is therefore given priority. This emphasis on the welfare of the individual does not, of course, deny the civic responsibilities and duties of each individual as a citizen in a democratic community; it merely sets these in proper perspective, as essential means to the greatest welfare of all the individuals in the community. Nor does it impugn the values of vocational and professional training; it merely assigns such training its proper place in the total pattern of instruction.

Formal instruction in a democracy must therefore be directed to three objectives—the welfare of each individual as an individual, responsible citizenship and political leadership, and vocational and professional competence. Primary importance is attached to the first of these objectives, but the importance of the second and third is also recognized. Liberal education is the only effective preparation for *both* the first and the second objective; vocational and professional training is requisite for the third. Ample provision must therefore be made in a democracy both for liberal education and for vocational and professional training, and their proper relationship must be maintained.

2. Education for the Good Life

(a) *The good life defined in terms of intrinsic values.* The phrase "the good life," which we have thus far used without definition, lends itself to sentimental and, indeed, vicious misuse. It is too often vaguely conceived and employed by people who have no adequate apprehension of its nature and implications. We can escape sentimentality and intellectual confusion by surveying human experience in its richest forms and by interpreting the good life in a significant cultural perspective. So approached, the content of the good life will be found to consist of those intrinsically satisfying experiences which sensitive and discriminating men and women, past and present, have found to be enriching and ennobling.

Men, cultures, and epochs have, of course, differed widely in basic interests and satisfactions. Indeed, no two individuals, social groups, or periods agree in all respects as to what is intrinsically satisfying. A democratic society seeks to recognize these differences, to permit their continuation, and even to promote them. Yet men also resemble one another in equally important ways. If history is in part a record of variety of experience, it is also a record of agreement on many basic issues. The good life, taken as a generic concept, must be defined in terms of this common factor.

How may this factor be most adequately described? What have all men, irrespective of race and creed, time and place, found to be intrinsically satisfying? The traditional answer to this question is still the most adequate. In its most thoughtful moments mankind has valued most highly the true, the good, and the beautiful. Truth, goodness, and beauty have been, and still continue to be, the objects of man's highest loyalty and the occasions of his deepest and most enduring satisfactions.

The terms "truth," "goodness," and "beauty," like the phrase "the good life," have been so misused and have acquired so many false and sentimental overtones that it is difficult to use them today without embarrassment. Yet since there are no adequate substitutes, and since their meanings are so basic, we shall continue to use them, explaining the meaning which we wish them to connote.

In the present context we shall employ them as omnibus terms to signify what is common to all specific instances of genuine insight, to all specific moral claims and responses, whether between man and man or between man and some higher power, and to all specific objects of aesthetic creation and aesthetic response.

Truth, goodness, and beauty also signify generic ideals. As such, they are inevitable points of reference. Whatever is regarded as true in a finite or relative sense is so regarded because it is judged to be a reasonable approximation to, or aspect of, the ideal of complete truth. To assert that a proposition is true necessarily involves a reference, however implicit, to truth in a more absolute sense, even though it must be admitted that human finitude precludes the possibility of our apprehending absolute truth in all its completeness. Absolute truth is the ideal aimed at in all honest inquiry, yet it must remain till the end of time only an ideal, since no finite mortal can ever wholly grasp it. The same applies to goodness and beauty. Both are ideals which man, by his very nature, is forever striving to reach but failing to attain completely.

This interpretation of truth, goodness, and beauty is one which some lay and professional philosophers today would criticize on the ground that, in our cognitive, moral, and aesthetic activities, we encounter only specific truths, instances of goodness, and beauties, and that, because of our inability adequately to envisage absolute ideals, we can assign no intelligible or useful meaning to them. Yet even philosophers of this persuasion will admit the intrinsic satisfaction which men, proportionately to their endowment, derive from concrete instances of cognitive, moral, and aesthetic activity. We therefore emphasize here what all particular instances of knowledge, goodness, and aesthetic satisfaction, respectively, have in common. We believe that all men attach intrinsic value to whatever insight they are capable of attaining; that all men judge aesthetic value to be intrinsically good and to require no further justification; and that all men regard love and friendship, respect for human dignity, allegiance to justice, and spiritual aspiration and dedication as good in themselves and of essential value to human life.

Variations in man's value judgments do not contradict the assertion that what men judge to be true, beautiful, and good seems to them to possess intrinsic value. Nor do these variations preclude the possibility of distinguishing between more adequate and less adequate appraisal, more or less informed opinion in these realms of value. Only the most ignorant and the most sophisticated would deny the possibility of being more or less enlightened in each of these types of human experience. Most men assume without question that there are many who are wiser than they are, and that some experts are superior to other experts, some artists to other artists, some critics to other critics, some moral leaders to other moral leaders. This assumption of the untutored is supported by the considered opinion of those who are themselves expert in one or other of these regions of human experience. In short, laymen and experts are in substantial agreement that the admission of human finitude does not commit us to a vicious relativism and to a skeptical abandonment of all standards of appraisal. Men do recognize the difference between more or less adequate insight, greater or less aesthetic perfection, and varying degrees of moral sensitivity; they do prefer the truer to the less true, the more beautiful to the less beautiful, and the morally better to the morally worse; and such recognition and preference imply no logical contradiction.

We are therefore justified in describing the good life in terms of maximum participation in these values, while recognizing that variations in native aptitude will result in more notable achievement by some individuals than by others, and that each individual will inevitably conceive of the good life in individual as well as generic terms.

Man's progressive realization of these ideals has always depended, and presumably always will depend, upon the effective preservation and transmission of his social and cultural heritage. Since human culture is a cumulative achievement, it depends upon the conservation of what man has accomplished and the effective introduction of each generation to this cultural tradition. The chief responsibility for its preservation and dissemination rests with the institutions best qualified to perform this task.

(b) *The school as one among many educational agencies.* Among educational institutions must be reckoned the family, church, press, radio, and motion picture, as well as the school. Each of these contributes greatly to education. The family excels in moral and social instruction, but it also contributes to the religious, intellectual, and aesthetic education of the growing child. The chief educational function of the church is religious and moral in character, but the church has also frequently promoted the discovery, and made possible the preservation, of secular truths (witness the Middle Ages) and has contributed greatly to man's artistic creation and enjoyment by stimulating and patronizing the arts. The press plays an important educative role, and more recently the motion picture and the radio have acquired, for better and for worse, an ever-increasing influence.

The school is therefore not solely responsible for education, and there is no reason to suppose that it will be able in the future to assume this enormous responsibility alone. The importance of formal education can be overemphasized. We are in danger of forgetting that other institutions must co-operate with the school if the larger end in view is to be achieved. Because of weaknesses in the church and the lack of discipline and cohesion in the family, we are sometimes tempted to urge the school to take over the responsibilities of the family and the church. Yet, if it attempts to perform, in addition to its own difficult and important function, any of the primary functions of these institutions, it will jeopardize its own distinctive contribution and become less effective in providing that type of education which it is best qualified to offer.

(c) *Liberal education the primary concern of the school.* The chief contribution of the school should be to provide opportunity for a liberal education. The function of a liberal education, in turn, is to increase both the breadth and the depth of man's experience of basic values. Our experience can be broadened and deepened, enriched and intensified, through the acquisition of new and profounder insight, finer moral discernment, and greater aesthetic sensitivity—in short, through the discovery and assimilation of new truths, beauties, and spiritual values. A liberal education is essentially an introduction to intrinsic values and cultural perspectives.

The primary objective of liberal education can also be defined as the acquisition of truth for its own sake. It is not the function of the school as a liberal institution to propagandize, to induce uncritical acceptance of dogmas. Nor is it its *primary* function to train man's creative impulses. The main task of liberal education is rather to promote understanding—understanding in every type of experience directly concerned with the good life. The habits which the teacher should cultivate in his students are those habits of thought and action which are essential to understanding, and the beliefs on which he has a right to insist are those which make possible the effective assimilation of old insights and the discovery of new insights. Since truth is expressed in many different forms and in different "languages" or media of communication, these differences should be taken into account, and the student should learn to understand these different languages and to share in different types of insight—scientific and artistic, moral and religious, historical and philosophical. No education is genuinely liberal which is restricted to only one region of human experience. But whatever the subject matter and approach, the main emphasis should always fall on understanding, on insights for their own sake, rather than on insights merely as a means to action and belief. Thus, a liberal education should include the study of religion as an historical phenomenon, a type of human experience, and a pattern of belief, and it should take into account variations in religious belief and practice as well as generic similarities; it should not demand acceptance of any specific religious beliefs or promote any specific religious practices. Its function is to enlighten, to promote understanding, not to proselytize. This applies not only to religion but to morality, art, and politics. In a democracy, it dare not even proselytize for democracy itself.

This emphasis on understanding does not, of course, deny the importance of commitment and action. Man must continually commit himself to beliefs in every field of human endeavor, and he must act on these beliefs. We must avoid the academic fallacy of defining the good life solely in terms of insight and understanding. Belief and action also are essential. But we must remember that liberal education contributes directly to belief and action by making them more informed and more reflective. It alone is able to free man from the tyranny of blindness and superstition and to safeguard him against the follies of unreflective behavior.

A certain type of commitment and action is essential to adequate apprehension. We cannot really understand a value situation without participating in it sympathetically as an "agent," that is, as one who is able to enter into the experience in question with some measure of assurance. Thus, certain religious insights are denied to those who find themselves unable to share in the requisite religious beliefs; the moral skeptic is debarred by his skepticism from entering sympathetically into the moral experience and from apprehending it from within; aesthetic understanding presupposes aesthetic enjoyment. Other types of insight can be acquired only through appropriate action. Actual participation in laboratory experiments, in artistic creation, in moral conduct, and in religious worship condition adequate comprehension. Yet here, as elsewhere, we must distinguish between means and ends and insist that the primary end of liberal education is insight. Truth is the value upon which liberal education must focus its chief attention if it is to preserve its integrity.

The "truth" here emphasized must not be narrowly restricted to what is mathematically or scientifically demonstrable, but must be taken to include reflective judgments in regions in which such demonstration is impossible. On questions of social theory and practice, artistic merit, and moral goodness, for example, mathematical certainty is unattainable and even scientific probability is beyond our reach. We can, however, hope to achieve in these regions the assurance which attaches to informed opinion. The alternative to rigorous demonstration is not sheer ignorance or blind faith; there is a middle region of opinion, and opinion can be more or less informed, assurance more or less adequately based on observation and reasonable interpretation. Liberal education, in its concern for truth, attaches as great importance to the best available insights and the wisest conclusions, where no rigorous demonstration is possible, as it does to the most assured demonstrations of the scientist and the mathematician. It endorses the Aristotelian demand for "as much clearness as the subject-matter admits of" and agrees with Aristotle that "it is the mark of an educated man to look for precision in each class of things just so far as the nature of the subject admits; it is evidently equally foolish to accept probable reasoning from a mathematician and to demand from a rhetorician scientific proof."[1]

3. Education for Citizenship and Political Leadership

In periods of tension political organizations lay particular emphasis upon unity and conformity, if not of thought, at least of behavior. In authoritarian states the political police are in the ascendancy; censorship and propaganda are intensively employed. Anxiety regarding the safety of the nation tends to produce parallel activities in a democracy. Thus from the earlier World War to the present there have been recurrent waves of emphasis

[1] *Ethica Nichomachea,* tr. W. D. Ross, 1094b.

upon "training" for democracy. Sometimes these have consisted of ritual cleansings of the outside of the cup. For example, children have been deprived of the right to attend school for failure, because of religious beliefs, to salute the flag. Teachers have been required to take oaths of loyalty, as though one who regarded religion as the opiate of the people would be deterred by an oath from subversive activities. In dealing with students, special courses of various kinds have been instituted. Mistaking procedure for process, many of these have substituted description for discipline. In others, facts have been supplied when faith was the conspicuous lack. Indeed, faith has often been weakened by criticisms based upon perfectionist wishes and utopian hopes, instead of strengthened by interpretations with historical perspective. In short, democracy has been wrongly interpreted as something for which one could be "trained" by superficial acquaintance with facts, by sentimental responses, by formal procedures and practices.

Our young people need to be educated in the democratic way of life. It is the duty of the school to have a share in this effort along with the home, the church, and other social forces. But special courses for that specific purpose tend to substitute dosage for hygiene, information for values; they attempt rapid and superficial results instead of developing deep understanding and of maturing impulses into habits appropriate to democracy. Training seeks, in short, to do directly and rapidly what can only be achieved, indirectly and slowly, by the educative process.

What type of instruction, then, will best lead to a realization of the rights and responsibilities of citizenship, to an appreciation and understanding of democracy? There is one way, and only one way, of fostering belief in democratic principles, and that is by developing the sensitivity of young people for the rights, obligations, and dignity of the individual, and by preparing them for freedom and the good life. Only through a realization of intrinsic values, of what truly constitutes the good life, can anyone be brought to understand the importance of democracy, for only as one believes in the innate dignity and the moral rights of the individual person can one truly believe in and support the democratic way of life.

Education for citizenship, accordingly, is identical with education for the good life. A liberal education is the only education for either objective. It alone provides the opportunity for participating in experiences of intrinsic value, and only through participation in them can one acquire understanding of the importance of the democratic form of government. It alone can give men the factual knowledge, the sense of basic values, the perspective and critical attitude, requisite to responsible citizenship.

A democracy requires not only an enlightened and socially minded citizenry; it also needs leaders able and willing to discharge the duties laid upon them. Such leaders must satisfy all the requirements for effective citizenship more completely than can be expected of the average voter. In a democracy the difference between the average citizen and the responsible statesman is a difference of degree, not of kind. Every citizen is under obligation to be, so far as possible, a statesman in his own right; every elected representative of the people is under obligation to exhibit the virtues of citizenship in an enhanced degree. He must be better informed than is the average voter, better able to understand basic issues by seeing them in larger perspective, more assured in his interpretation of those ultimate values to which a democracy is dedicated.

It follows that, whereas some measure of liberal education is essential to ordinary citizenship in a democracy, more education of the same type is essential to enlightened leadership in a democratic society. The outstanding leaders in our democracy have been men of unusual political and social vision, and this vision has been the evidence of a liberally educated mind. Our wisest statesmen achieved, during their formative years, a sound liberal education, formal or informal, and this education contributed largely to their proficiency as statesmen. We shall need liberally educated leaders in the future fully as much as we have needed them in the past.

4. Training in Specific Vocations and Professions

A differentiation between liberal education and vocational or professional training need not imply that man's life as an individual citizen and his vocational or professional pursuits should be divorced from each other, or that the two corresponding forms of instruction are wholly unrelated to each other. The very reverse is true. These two aspects of human activity are intimately related, and the two types of instruction should certainly complement each other. Liberal education has led directly into certain professions and has provided a basis for greater success in all the professions and vocations; vocational and professional interests have often motivated liberal inquiry. Recognition of these interrelationships, however, does not lessen the desirability of distinguishing between education and training.

Most men and an increasing number of women today earn their living. The more technical vocations require considerable specialized training, as do the more responsible and interesting professions. The school cannot ignore its responsibility to provide such vocational and professional training; our young people have the right to whatever specialized preparation for life their aptitudes and interests dictate. How should such training be related to liberal education?

There are many young people in our schools whose natural endowment enables them to achieve, even under the most favorable circumstances, only a limited measure of liberal education. They should therefore be encouraged to start their vocational training fairly early and helped to prepare themselves for some interesting and useful vocation. Our schools are performing this service with increasing efficiency and have reason to be proud of their record.

In our enthusiasm for vocational training, however, we must remember that a liberal education has values even for those who cannot fully participate in its benefits. Even a partial liberal education is valuable, and, in a sense, the more necessary, the more routine and mechanized the vocational activities of the individual in question. In our industrial age more and more people are having to spend their working hours in types of activity so largely regimented and mechanical as to provide no adequate outlet for individual judgment and initiative, imagination or critical reflection. With the reduction of working hours, increased leisure is opening the way to cultural and humane avocations. The growing adult education movement in this country is offering an increasing number of people valuable aid and encouragement along these lines. Whatever the school can do to educate our citizens of varying capacities for a more rewarding use of leisure is clearly of great human importance.

On the other hand, many young people have a natural endowment which should enable them to occupy positions of responsibility in our society. It is to their own interest and to the public interest to postpone specialized training as long as possible, and to acquire during their formative years a broad and firm educational foundation. Young people of this type should be reminded that a liberal education is an essential condition of fullest effectiveness, and that premature and too narrow specialization will handicap them in their profession. The more challenging the job, the greater the need for perspective and adaptability to new situations, and this need can be met only through appropriate development of the mind and the imagination.

Specialized activity, whether vocational, and therefore narrow and restricted in scope, or professional, and therefore more inclusive and challenging, is by definition not self-sufficient. Just as statesmanship demands that specialized activity be guided by a larger wisdom, so should vocational and professional activity be motivated and directed by an allegiance to intrinsically satisfying objectives. Man cannot live as a human being by his vocation or profession alone; his vocational and professional activities will be humanly oriented only if he can pursue them with a pervading sense of human values. Many of the dislocations of our society have been occasioned by specialists who have engaged in their specialized activities with technical competence but without adequate realization of the place which such activities should occupy in their own lives or in the society of which they are members.

5. The Good Life, Democracy, and Liberal Education

It is evident that the good life is related to democracy and liberal education as ultimate end to necessary means, and that democracy and education, in turn, mutually condition each other. The members of a mature social group can participate in the good life most richly in a democracy, and liberal education is essential for the full realization of human potentialities. Thus democracy and education are both merely means to an ultimate end. But their importance as means is very great.

That democracy and liberal education mutually condition each other is equally clear. Democracy can function only in a society of reasonably mature and enlightened citizens, and maturity and enlightenment can be achieved only through the agency of liberal education. Such education, in turn, is available to the common man only in a democracy. The authoritarian state cannot afford to let any citizen search for the truth wherever the search may lead. Only in a democratic state is the luxury of free speech and untrammeled inquiry possible, and these "luxuries" are, from the democratic point of view, not luxuries at all but prime necessities, because without them a democracy cannot flourish.

Inevitably, in a society as youthful as ours, as impatient with tradition and as economic in orientation, liberal education is conceived by many people as a mere luxury, and by some as an activity hardly worthy of serious attention or support. Our purpose here is to show that any tendency to neglect liberal education threatens our culture and our democratic way of life. We urge, with all the emphasis at our command, that liberal education, wisely conceived, must be accorded an essential place in our society if the democratic spirit is to flourish and grow strong, and if American citizens are to have the opportunity to achieve the good life as richly as their native endowments permit. Far from being of mere "academic" interest, the issues here are of national importance. They are of importance to all teachers and scholars, to every thoughtful citizen, both in his private capacity and as a citizen enjoying the rights and obligations of the franchise, to all who are entrusted with governmental authority. We shall succeed in preserving our democracy only so long as we deserve to do so and only if we are able to demonstrate to a hostile world our ability to make it really work. And we can make it work only if we are sufficiently enlightened, as American citizens, to participate in government in a wise and responsible manner, and sufficiently educated, as individuals, to share in the good life to the limit of our several abilities.

Chapter 4. THE CONTENT OF A LIBERAL EDUCATION

If we assume that the chief end of liberal education is the promotion of the good life, that is, the richest possible participation in intrinsic values, what should be the form and content of such education? What subjects are of sufficient cultural importance to merit inclusion in a liberal program of study? How should these subjects be studied and taught in a liberal institution? What habits of mind and what instruments are necessary to the exploration of these subjects?

These questions invite an historical investigation into the development of the liberal arts and sciences, and a reconsideration of such basic problems as the nature of knowledge, the conditions of wise evaluation, and the sources of intrinsic satisfaction. No such inquiry can be attempted here. We must restrict ourselves to an examination of the chief disciplines now included in most liberal arts curricula and to a consideration of the contribution which each of these disciplines can reasonably be expected to make to a rich and integrated liberal education.

The conclusion which we believe this investigation will sustain is that each of the major liberal disciplines has an essential contribution to make, but that none is of such a character and importance as to justify exclusive emphasis upon it at the expense of the others. Each will be found to have its own distinctive values and limitations; none can be ignored with impunity, and none should be allowed to monopolize the attention of the student.

We shall analyze these disciplines in terms of their relation to truth, goodness, and beauty, because we believe that the individual can best weave this great "threefold cord" into his own life with the aid of these liberal disciplines.

Truth, as we have seen, occupies a unique position, since all disciplines are primarily dedicated to the preservation of insights already achieved, the discovery of new insights, and the dissemination of whatever truth is at any given time available to man. In this sense a liberal education is the pursuit of "truth for truth's sake," whatever the subject or field of investigation. This does not mean, however, that a liberal curriculum is indifferent to beauty and goodness or that liberal studies are ineffectual in the promotion of goodness and hostile to artistic creation. Each of the liberal disciplines, though some much more directly than others, can promote moral sensitivity and understanding. They can do so because true morality involves knowledge and a respect for imaginative insight and informed sympathy. They should discourage mechanical acceptance of specific patterns of belief and conduct, blind obedience, and mere conventional goodness. But they should help to arouse and strengthen moral attitudes and encourage moral behavior. Similarly, though the study of the arts and literatures is directly concerned with beauty in the several media, other liberal disciplines, such as mathematics and the sciences, are not indifferent to aesthetic quality. Thus the liberal disciplines, though concerned primarily with truth and the conditions of its discovery and apprehension, are genuinely concerned with beauty and goodness. It is necessary to hold in mind this tripartite division in order to keep in clear focus the ultimate relation between liberal education and the good life, conceived of in terms of the three intrinsic values.

Our attention must be directed solely to the nature and function of these disciplines as liberal studies; we shall not discuss their utilitarian application. Mathematics is essential to engineering and industry, and the natural sciences have contributed enormously to our health and comfort. But these utilitarian contributions would not of themselves justify the inclusion of these subjects in a liberal curriculum.

On the other hand, the disciplines which merit inclusion in a liberal program do so not merely because of their immediate bearing on specific truths, beauties, and instances of goodness and their direct contribution to the good life, but also because of functions which, though liberal in character, are mediate and secondary. Thus, the natural sciences are primarily valuable as liberal studies for the knowledge they give us of the structure of the physical universe. They merit inclusion in a liberal curriculum, however, because they also offer such excellent discipline in careful observation and objective interpretation— a discipline essential to the search for truth in any field of inquiry. Similarly, the liberal study of the arts and literatures not only contributes to our understanding and appreciation of artistic beauties and insights but, in addition, strengthens and disciplines the imagination, which is essential to moral and religious comprehension. We shall therefore distinguish in what follows between the primary and the secondary functions of the liberal disciplines.

1. *Mathematics*

The most abstract of the liberal disciplines is pure mathematics. It is the study of pure form; it concerns itself entirely with abstract entities, relationships, and operations. Since it is not bound to empirical data, it is free to ignore the world of nature and to explore the realm of mathematical possibility. That mathematical systems are frequently given "interpretations" that make them applicable to nature, as in the case of arithmetic and geometry, does not alter the fact that pure mathematics concerns itself with pure mathematical structure.

The component parts of a mathematical system stand to one another in the relation of strict implication; a mathematical structure is thus *a priori* in character. By this is meant that certain given or assumed premises are found to imply with complete logical rigor certain conclusions which are implicit in them. The process by which these implications are discovered is deductive reasoning.

(a) *Primary function.* The realm of the mathematical *a priori* has fascinated man for many centuries, and the working out of mathematical relationships has been one of the most stimulating, revealing, and successful of human activities. It is easy to see why mathematical precision has been the ideal of the natural sciences, and even occasionally of philosophy. Since the purpose of a liberal education is to introduce the student to all the great fields of human inquiry, mathematics must be given an important place in a liberal curriculum.

(b) *Secondary functions.* A person wisely instructed in mathematics will also value what is sometimes called mathematical "elegance." A demonstration in mathematics is said to be "elegant" when it exemplifies a fine economy of means. It is always possible to demonstrate a theorem more or less directly, to employ mathematical notions and operations more or less felicitously, and to exhibit to a greater or a less degree mathematical originality, imaginative power, and intuitive penetration. The greater the success along these lines, the greater the resulting "elegance" and the attendant aesthetic satisfaction. The importance of this factor is seldom recognized by the layman in mathematics. Yet expert mathematicians insist that "elegance" is of great concern to them as mathematicians and not an irrelevant satisfaction. It is particularly evident in the higher reaches of pure mathematics, but it is also already discernible in more elementary mathematics, for example, in plane geometry. A student who remains blind to this factor cannot be said to have an adequate comprehension of mathematical theory or to have derived from his study of mathematics as a liberal discipline the fullest benefit and enjoyment.

The study of mathematics has often been recommended for its disciplinary value as "mental training." This raises a debatable issue. Can exercise in precise mathematical thinking promote accurate thinking in other subjects? Discussion of this problem has usually not been conducted at a sufficiently high level of generality; "transference" has been defended and attacked in too narrow and mechanical a fashion. The crucial fact is that man's basic mental processes are essentially the same, whatever the specific subject matter upon which they are focused. Precise analysis, valid inference, cogent synthesis, intuitive insight— these activities, however diverse in application to specific problems in different fields, have a common character. It is this fundamental identity of basic mental process which endows rigorous exercise in any field with a wider significance, and which gives such exercise its disciplinary value.

If this be granted, effective instruction in mathematical reasoning is simultaneously instruction in abstract reasoning as such. Familiarity with the rigor and precision of mathematical demonstration establishes standards of rigor and precision for all deductive demonstration. The student who has learned what can and cannot be derived from mathematical premises has thereby received a discipline in logical inference which he can apply in all situations in which logical inference is relevant.

If mathematical instruction is really to provide such mental discipline, however, the subject must be so taught that the nature of deduction from given premises, of consistency and coherence, of avoidance of contradiction and *non sequitur,* is driven home. If it is taught merely as an accumulation of formulae to be memorized, with no attention to the pattern of reasoning itself, the student can hardly be expected to apply to non-mathematical problems a competence derived from his mathematical studies. The fault in this case cannot be laid at the door of mathematics as such, but must be attributed to the manner in which it has been taught and learned. A secondary function of mathematical education is therefore a general mental discipline which justifies the inclusion of mathematics in a liberal curriculum.

Another secondary function of mathematics is obvious and need only be mentioned. Other liberal disciplines rely so heavily upon mathematical methods that they cannot be studied without some use of mathematics. This is especially true of the natural sciences, but the social studies also find statistical analysis increasingly important. The study of mathematics is thus a prerequisite to various other liberal disciplines. This is an added reason for including mathematics in a liberal curriculum.

2. *The Natural Sciences*

The natural sciences have in common an interest in the world of "fact" as contrasted with the realm of "values." This distinction between "fact" and "value" does not deny the reality or objectivity of values; it merely marks the well-recognized difference between value and non-value situations. The pure sciences are descriptive and explanatory rather than evaluative; their interpretations are concerned with the structure and behavior of natural phenomena rather than with their significance for man. Relying upon a distinctive type of observation, experimentation, and interpretation, they attempt to lay bare the regularities and irregularities which characterize events in space and time. No matter what he is studying, the scientist maintains his objective and external approach, and he applies his criteria of scientific judgment in all cases alike. Students of the arts and literatures, morality and religion, in contrast, must enter sympathetically into value experiences and attempt to set up standards of appraisal. We shall return to this distinction at a later point in the discussion.

The biological and physical sciences, including those which study human beings as psycho-physical organisms, may be considered together because every science attempts to investigate its subject matter with the same basic methods and the same large end in view, that is, the discovery and symbolic representation of the regularities and irregularities of natural phenomena. The natural sciences resemble mathematics in their concern for precision and their preoccupation with quantitive variations. It is this characteristic which makes them dependent upon mathematics. They differ from mathematics primarily in their continual reference to the actually existing world of nature. The ultimate goal of all scientific inquiry is the more adequate understanding of the structures and processes of nature. This all-important orientation to nature is the new factor which emerges as we pass from pure mathematics to the pure natural sciences.

(a) *Primary function*. The primary function of the sciences in a liberal curriculum is to introduce the student to man's cumulative scientific insights and to scientific problems which still await solution. The scientist puts at our disposal a knowledge of nature's complexity, regularity, and diversity which is fascinating to an alert mind. He opens our eyes to the permanent and the transitory, to the infinitely great, the infinitely small, and the infinitely old. In no field of inquiry has more been done during the past centuries to fire man's imagination, whet his curiosity, and instill in him the desire to participate in the search for new truths or to share vicariously in the achievements of others. A student who completes his formal education without being introduced to this exciting intellectual adventure has forfeited an important part of his cultural heritage.

(b) *Secondary function.* In discussing the secondary function of the natural sciences as liberal disciplines we will ignore their utilitarian value. No doubt it is somewhat arbitrary to attempt to draw a sharp line between pure and applied science, since so much new and important scientific knowledge is continually emerging from the pursuits of the applied scientist. Here, as elsewhere, theory and practice, knowledge and its application, cannot be divorced without the danger of distortion. Nonetheless, it is pure science as an experimental and theoretical discipline, and not science in its innumerable practical applications, which merits the special attention of those primarily interested in liberal education.

We have pointed out that mathematics promotes understanding of, and respect for, *logical coherence.* Science promotes a similar understanding of, and respect for, *correspondence to fact.* The natural sciences are, of course, also loyal to the ideal of logical coherence, but, as has been indicated, this ideal can best be appreciated in the study of mathematics. In science priority is assigned to correspondence to fact in the sense that when a scientific theory conflicts with a verified observation or fact, the theory, even though internally consistent, must be modified or abandoned. No scientific theory can survive a single well-established fact to which it cannot accommodate itself.

There is good reason to believe that discipline in scientific inquiry is of value in other types of inquiry. The effective study of one science is certainly an appreciable aid to the study of another science, for "scientific method" is essentially the same in all the sciences. The astronomer approaches his problems with the same attitude and ideals as the physiologist, however different their subject matter, instruments, and specialized techniques. But respect for correspondence to fact is also important in the non-scientific disciplines. This respect, when awakened by the study of natural science, is available to other kinds of investigation. Science thus offers a valuable discipline in objective, as opposed to subjective, or wishful, thinking. One of man's strongest tendencies is to escape from reality, to refuse to face facts or think about them as clearly as possible, to believe what he would like to believe rather than what observation and reason justify. The sciences provide a discipline in precise objective thinking and a corrective for subjectivism and sentimentality. Whoever believes that it is more honest to face facts than to ignore them, and to interpret facts in a rational rather than an irrational manner, will value particularly this general contribution of science to man's intellectual and spiritual integrity.

3. *The Social Studies*

The studies here in question are economics, political science, anthropology, sociology, and the like. Their generic subject matter is man in society. Students in this field are interested in all social phenomena, in everything that concerns man's corporate activities. Some of the social studies concentrate their attention upon specific types of social activity and organization. The economist, for example, is primarily interested in the factor of wealth and other related factors in society; the political scientist, in governmental structure and activity. Other social studies are more inclusive in their interest. The anthropologist concerns himself with every aspect of primitive societies, the sociologist, with the structures and functions of society as such.

There is probably more dispute over the goals and methods of these studies and their actual and potential value than in most of the other academic disciplines. This is because human nature is so complex and because the social disciplines are relatively undeveloped. Man's individual and corporate behavior can, indeed, be studied somewhat in the way in which natural phenomena are studied in the natural sciences. But man is not *merely* a part of nature. His behavior differs in essential respects from the behavior of other animate beings, for he can act purposively, and consciously seek to realize ideal ends. No adequate understanding of society is possible without due recognition of this distinctively human trait.

The investigator in this field may be called a "scientist" in so far as he seeks to maintain toward his subject matter an attitude of scientific impartiality, and to devise methods of investigation which resemble those of the natural sciences in precision. Social groups do not, indeed, lend themselves to investigation by the experimental method, and this fact imposes a severe limitation upon the social scientist. Nonetheless, social phenomena do manifest regularities and divergencies which can be isolated, recorded, and interpreted with some precision. Statistical and other methods of investigation are being devised which may also enable us in time to understand certain factors in social behavior sufficiently well to make possible a type of prediction and control at present beyond our reach. Whatever the inadequacies of the social "sciences" today, therefore, and however little they may at present merit this designation, they are, at least in these respects, "scientific" in character.

Since, however, the social disciplines dare not ignore human values and objectives, their strictly scientific observations and interpretations must fall short of comprehensive adequacy. They cannot hope to progress even at the theoretical level unless man's evaluations and efforts to realize ideal ends are fully recognized. Progress in social theory must depend essentially upon the ability of the student of society to take these human objectives into account. He must be wise in his appreciation of human values if he is to achieve a true understanding of social institutions and behavior.

It is precisely here, in the realm of value, that the social disciplines merge with the humanistic disciplines. Since the latter explicitly concern themselves with values and make it their business to understand and interpret man's artistic, moral, and religious insights, they provide the complementary approach to the study of man. It is not the primary task of the social disciplines to establish human ends. They can utilize man's humanistic insights in determining the actual and ideal ends of human endeavor, just as they can derive from the natural sciences suggestions as to relevant methods for the discovery of social means productive of these ends. Accordingly, theirs is in many ways a mediating role; their task is to combine man's spiritual and scientific insights and to show how both contribute to the understanding and solution of social problems.

We have thus far said nothing about history as one of the social studies. It is clear that none of these studies can afford to neglect the temporal dimension. To understand the contemporary scene the student of society must be able to see it in historical perspective and know the evolution of social patterns and concepts. Modern economic theory, for example, cannot neglect economic practices and theories of earlier centuries, nor can political science ignore the political structures and theories of other periods. Some of the natural sciences are not greatly dependent upon an historical perspective, though it might be argued that even a scientist cannot fully appreciate the significance of modern science save by viewing it in the light of its historical development. But the social studies are peculiarly dependent upon a knowledge of history because their subject matter, human society, is essentially embedded in the time process.

Hence, the greater the autonomy of the various social studies, the greater the obligation of each to provide its own historical orientation. At present these disciplines rely largely on history, conceived as a separate discipline, to supply the temporal perspective. We shall consider at the end of this chapter the more inclusive function of history as a synthesizing discipline. Here attention is directed merely to its more limited task of tracing the evolution of social phenomena. History conceived of in these terms is indeed one of the social studies and one which stands in a peculiar relation to the rest. Its function is to complement their predominantly analytical and systematic approach; it explores the temporal dimension of society, whereas they tend to emphasize recurrent regularities and types of behavior.

The work of the historian complements that of the social scientist in another respect, namely, in focusing sharply upon individual persons, events, and patterns in human history. The tendency of science is always to move from individual phenomena to universal laws, and to regard phenomena as specific manifestations of these laws. In this sense the scientist is interested ultimately in the general rather than the particular, the law rather than its particular embodiment. This tendency, though perhaps not so pronounced as in natural science, is evident also in the social disciplines. The historian can do much to complement this emphasis by his insistence on historical individuality and uniqueness. He too, of course, is interested in whatever recurrences he can discover in the course of history, but this interest is always accompanied by, and often subordinated to, an interest in the individuality of historical phenomena, large and small.

History in the narrower sense has, then, its own subject matter and approach and its own methods of investigation, verification, and interpretation. Its subject matter is the temporal evolution of social phenomena, and these are studied with regard to their individuality as well as their more universal character. Its methods are essentially the same as those of historians in other fields such as philosophy, art, and religion. But historical research in these fields is continually indebted to the professional historian in the more limited sense, not only for specific historical facts and interpretations but for a progressive refinement of historical method. In short, the scholars who are entitled "historians" have their own interests and problems, but their primary concern with social phenomena justifies the classification of history, in this sense, among the social disciplines.

(a) *Primary function.* What, then, is the primary function of the social studies as liberal disciplines, and what place do they deserve in a liberal curriculum? The problems with which they deal are as intrinsically interesting as are the problems of any of the other liberal disciplines, and the insights to which they lead are as significant as are new insights in other fields of inquiry. It is as important to know how men behave, and have behaved, in social groups, and how they have organized and are now organizing themselves to achieve certain ends as it is to know the structure and behavior of natural phenomena. Since these investigations have been so largely neglected until recent times, the effort today to make them more precise, objective, and dispassionate is encouraging. A knowledge of available facts and pertinent theories concerning social structure and behavior, a familiarity with the increasingly specialized methods and techniques of the social disciplines, and a recognition of basic social problems and their significance for human life must certainly be accorded a place in a liberal education.

(b) *Secondary functions.* Their chief secondary function is to provide a social orientation for the other liberal disciplines. The arts and sciences, moral and religious beliefs and practices, can be understood only in a wider social context. The anthropologist adds to our understanding of these aspects of human life by describing their earliest manifestations in primitive cultures and their relation, in these cultures, to other human activities and needs. The historian, in surveying the social, political, and economic structures and forces of various cultures and periods, provides the other disciplines with an essential historical setting. The sociologist attempts to interpret the varied aspects of a society in their relation to one another, and thus to do justice to the organic nature of society as such. The economist and the political scientist put at our disposal various specific facts and theories which contribute greatly to our understanding of the arts and sciences. In short, the social disciplines illumine various aspects of society which have influenced, and been influenced by, artistic, scientific, moral, and religious thought and practice.

It is important to clarify the disciplinary value which social studies at present do and do not possess. Even in their relatively undeveloped state they help the student, even more effectively than do any of the other disciplines, to escape prejudice and a blinding emotionalism on social issues. Wisely taught, they foster in him a catholicity of outlook and a judicious restraint in his consideration of conflicting patterns of belief and modes of behavior. The need for such a discipline today is peculiarly urgent. It is important to help the student to respect informed opinion in this field and to make his own opinions more informed and objective.

On the other hand, the social studies cannot compete with pure mathematics and the natural sciences in exhaustive analysis, rigorous inference, or verifiable interpretation. Their methods are by nature such as to forbid the substitution of these studies for the more precise and established disciplines. The latter must continue to supply a distinctive and fundamental type of exercise in consistent reasoning and fidelity to empirical data.

4. *The Humanities*

The humanities, unlike the sciences, are primarily concerned with values and critical appraisal. Since their subject matter is man's experiences of value and his ideals and standards, they are directed to what is most intimately and peculiarly human. The disciplines usually entitled the "humanities" concern themselves with the apprehension, analysis, and interpretation of expressed insights in the realms of morality, religion, art and literature. In so far as history and philosophy concern themselves with these insights, they too must be included among the humanistic disciplines.

Before we can discuss the essential nature and liberal functions of these disciplines, we must consider briefly the special role of language in all humanistic studies and the distinctive contributions which the study of language can make in this field.

A. *The nature and study of language*

The role of language in humanistic studies is analogous to the role of mathematics in the natural sciences. Language, taken generically to include all vehicles of communication, non-verbal as well as verbal, is obviously essential for the expression of man's moral, religious, or artistic insights. No insight in these realms can be understood by anyone ignorant of the medium in which it is expressed. This is as true of the fine arts as of literature; the first task of the student of the fine arts is to learn the "languages," including the "grammar" and "syntax," of the several media in their successive stylistic and cultural manifestations. But the verbal languages derive a peculiar importance from the fact that they are in universal use in all social intercourse, and also from the fact that they are the natural and most effective vehicle for innumerable humanistic insights. In the following consideration of language we shall, therefore, limit our discussion to the verbal languages and their study.

A vital function of the study of a foreign language is to impart the ability to read works of literary merit in the original. It is a truism that foreign literatures cannot be fully appreciated by one whose knowledge of the language employed is deficient. Something can no doubt be preserved in a translation. But the appreciation of literary values and insights must be direct; it must be achieved in and through the actual medium employed. Much that is precious is lost in reading a translation, and the more perfect the literary composition, the greater the loss both in form and in content. The tendency today to minimize this loss is a sad reflection on a widespread insensitivity to literary values and an indifference to the precise expression of ideas. Only a person with very deficient taste could accept with complacence the compulsion to read the great ancient and modern classics in translation.

It is obvious that a reading knowledge of French and German is also a requisite to competence in any of the liberal disciplines, that a knowledge of Italian and Spanish is invaluable in some fields, and that Greek and Latin are essential in many intellectual enterprises, particularly in the humanities. Our graduate students and younger scholars who have received an inadequate linguistic training in school and college are giving increasing evidence of how seriously they are handicapped by this deficiency.

The study of Greek and Latin has a special value in increasing an American student's understanding of his own language. English in its earlier stages was essentially like Latin and Greek in its use of inflection, or the forms of words, as practically the sole method of indicating grammatical relationships. Throughout its history, English has gradually substituted other grammatical methods for the single device of inflections. Word order, for example, which was formerly simply connotative, has now become an important method of showing certain grammatical relationships. But the use of inflections in a few functions still continues in English. The study of Greek and Latin provides one of the best introductions to the role of inflection in our grammatical methods and, by contrast, to an understanding of the functions of the other devices we now use in place of inflections. Greek and Latin are to be preferred to other inflectional languages because of the contribution which has been made to our cultural heritage through these languages. This cultural heritage shows itself not only in nearly every aspect of the material of our art and literature and thought, but also in a large portion of our vocabulary—notably in the so-called learned words. Although many of these words have now certain semantic values that were foreign to their use in their original settings, still an experience with these words in contexts of Greek and Latin thought provides an insight into their functioning in English which no other experience can give. Greek and Latin are to be preferred also not only because of their cultural contribution to the whole of Western civilization, but because, on the one hand, of the special relation to all the Romance languages which have derived from Latin and, on the other hand, of the particular place which these languages hold in relation to the whole Indo-European family of languages to which English belongs and from which it derives its essential structure.

Full recognition of the value of studying foreign languages, ancient and modern, should not preclude equal recognition of the value of studying English grammar and syntax. This study is facilitated by a knowledge of those languages, other than Greek and Latin, from which English derives many of its words and constructions. But the English language has its own distinctive characteristics, which deserve far more explicit study than has been accorded them. Recent work in semantics focused upon the English language as such is rapidly demonstrating the value of this approach.

The importance of language in general as a vehicle for thought and communication is obvious. Since thought depends essentially upon a medium, we cannot think clearly unless we have at our disposal a language adequate to the articulation of our ideas. The sad inability of many American students to clarify their own thinking and to express themselves with precision is to a considerable extent the result of their lack of an adequate verbal medium. They simply do not possess the verbal equipment which they need to achieve that degree of intellectual clarity which they might otherwise attain. And the notorious inability of the average

American student to read good English prose and poetry with precision and comprehension—an inability amply demonstrated by recent studies—is in large measure the result of his inadequate mastery of language in general and of his mother tongue in particular. We are, as a nation, so largely inarticulate, and our thinking is so sentimental and banal, partly because our schools and colleges are failing to give our young people the linguistic training to which they are entitled.

The rigorous study of language, like the study of mathematics, has fundamental values available for other disciplines. Excessive claims have indeed been made for such study, and the various languages have frequently been taught in a mechanical and unenlightened manner, with major emphasis on sheer memory. When languages are taught, however, with proper emphasis on linguistic structure and the meaning of words, that is, on syntactical usage and semantic reference, such study is invaluable in clarifying meanings and promoting precise expression.

The study of language for its own sake is also somewhat analogous to the study of mathematics for its own sake. The structure of a language is so intricate, linguistic meanings are so subtle, and the evolution of a language and its relation to other languages can be traced with such precision that the study of language as such has its peculiar fascination for the informed student. When account is also taken of the intimate relation between a language and its culture, with its distinctive *Weltanschauung*, and of the factor of linguistic "elegance," comparable to mathematical "elegance," it is easy to see why language study has been and still is an engrossing humanistic activity.

The danger against which we must be on guard in our colleges and universities, particularly at the graduate level, is that of an uninformed and pedantic centering on language minutiae as matters of antiquarian interest only, of a philology that treats literary masterpieces without ever bringing its learning to bear upon the work as literature with artistic values and expressed meanings. The opposite danger, which is just as real, is that of neglecting rigorous linguistic study in a premature enthusiasm for artistic form and for the ideas thus expressed. There are many "humanists" who have given linguistics scant attention and who would be much better humanists had they applied themselves more conscientiously to it as an essential humanistic discipline.

B. *The arts and literatures*

The subject matter of the "humanities" (in the narrower sense) is the aggregate of all "works of art" in the several artistic media. ("Art" is here taken to include literature as well as the so-called "fine arts.") A work of art has two major aspects which must be kept in mind. It has, on the one hand, an "aesthetic surface" which is the object of immediate aesthetic response and the occasion of aesthetic delight. Since this surface is always an organization of a medium, that is, a pattern of distinguishable aesthetic elements, and since beauty is usually conceived of as a function of formal structure, this aspect of the work of art may be entitled its "beauty."

The beauty of a work of art, however, does not exhaust its nature. A work of art is also a vehicle of communication, for art is the expression, through beauty or artistic form, of the artist's interpretation of some aspect of human experience or of the world which constitutes man's environment. Recognition of what the artist has to "say" in a work of art, that is, of his expressed insights, need not involve any neglect of the importance of art's aesthetic surface or of the pure aesthetic satisfaction which it occasions. For not only do beauty in all its forms and aesthetic delight in all its manifestations possess intrinsic value; the artist can give artistic expression to his insights only in and through artistic form, by making the fullest use of the aesthetic surface of his art as an expressive vehicle.

The nature of art can also be indicated by describing, however briefly, two characteristics of artistic creation which differentiate it from scientific research. In the first place, the artist's approach to reality, unlike that of the scientist, is essentially evaluative. He is always concerned with the significance of his subject matter for man and with the meaning of human experience. His approach to reality is never cold, impersonal, and dispassionate. Art, at its best, exhibits unusual sympathetic insight. The artist is distinguished from other men by his pre-eminent ability to discern, with imaginative power, what the average man apprehends only feebly and confusedly. The arts are therefore the most effective vehicle at man's disposal for the apprehension and communication of whatever endows human experience with significance.

The artist is distinguished, in the second place, by the role of individuality in all his artistic endeavor. His approach to life and reality is always a highly individual approach, and he expresses his interpretation of his subject matter in a work of art which is itself highly individual. This dual emphasis upon individuality, however, by no means precludes the universality of art. For the greater the work of art, the more universal are its expressed insights—the more successfully does it portray and illumine the man in men, that is, those aspects of human experience and those abiding truths which men can understand and share. Homer and Shakespeare, Michelangelo and Beethoven, are individual in their approach to life, and their artistic products are individual works of art; but what these works express remains intelligible and significant through the centuries.

The disciplines which concern themselves with the arts study them from various complementary points of view. Their approach is, in the first place, historical. Here the attempt is made to investigate individual works of art and specific styles in an historical perspective, to interpret them in their social and cultural context, and to consider the ways in which artists, schools, and movements have influenced one another. These historical investigations include more specialized studies such as archaeology, iconography, epigraphy, and the like. They also take into account relevant biographical material. The art historian considers as relevant to his work all historical data and interpretations which throw light on the nature of art in different cultures and successive periods.

The historical approach is complemented by the analytical and systematic approach, which is usually undertaken by the more philosophically minded students of art. Here attention is directed to the distinctive media of the several arts, that is, to the "languages," verbal and non-verbal, of artistic expression; to artistic form, that is, generic patterns and the structure of individual works of art; and, finally, to the analysis of artistic content, that is, of what is expressed by individual artists and by artistic schools and movements.

Another task of the humanities is that of sensitive interpretation of individual works of art in their uniqueness. Here the effort is to recapture as far as possible the experiences and insights of the artist. This "re-creative" task can be accomplished successfully only with the aid of appropriate historical orientation, analytical scrutiny, and genuine aesthetic sensitivity.

The student of art must also attempt an understanding appraisal. It is his responsibility to assess, to the best of his ability, the aesthetic merit of the works of art with which he concerns himself and to consider their human significance.

These various approaches to the work of art indicate the complexity of artistic criticism. It is at once historical and systematic, re-creative and evaluative. The complexity of the total enterprise has inevitably led to specialization. Students of the arts have increasingly become specialists in one or another field or aspect of humanistic study. Yet it is clear that no one approach is independent of the other approaches, and that an adequate understanding of art must presuppose some measure of competence along all these lines.

(a) *Primary function.* A primary function of these "humanistic" disciplines is to cultivate the student's taste, to sharpen his eye and his ear, to promote his artistic discernment, and thus to increase his capacity for aesthetic delight. Men differ, no doubt, in native aesthetic ability, but all men have some innate endowment for aesthetic response and each individual can, with suitable exercise, develop his native aptitude and acquire the capacity for more deeply satisfying aesthetic enjoyment. A young person who has not been introduced to works of art, and who has not been taught to observe and to enjoy their aesthetic character to the limit of his ability, has been deprived of an important part of his cultural heritage and has been condemned to a life less rich than it might otherwise have been.

The "humanistic" disciplines are especially important because they put at the student's disposal the insights of the great artists. Were the meaning of a work of art self-evident to the completely untutored observer, the "humanities" would not have this important function. But this is not the case. Historical orientation, analysis, sensitive re-creation, and a developed taste are all essential to an adequate understanding and appreciation of what a work of art is and what the artist is attempting to convey to us. The final goal of all teaching in the "humanities" is to promote such understanding and response, and only as this task is competently performed are the insights of the great artists made available to the student.

There is a growing recognition in this country that much can be learned about the arts from actual participation in the act of artistic creation. It is important, however, to define clearly that type of education in the creative arts which should be included in a liberal arts curriculum. It is not the function of such a curriculum to provide instruction in the artistic techniques or to promote artistic creation for their own sake. There is a place in a liberal arts program, however, for instruction in the creative arts which is designed to increase the student's understanding of art and the artistic process. Wise teaching along these lines can undoubtedly result in opening the student's eyes and ears to aspects of the arts to which he would otherwise remain blind and deaf. The attempt, however amateurish, actually to paint a picture, write a sonnet, compose a song, or model a figure in clay, is a valuable complement to the scholarly and re-creative approaches. But instruction in the creative arts has a place in a liberal arts program only so long as it positively contributes to the student's understanding of the arts, for it is understanding upon which the major liberal emphasis must fall.

A liberal study of the arts and literatures will help a student to escape at least in some measure from aesthetic prejudice and to achieve a greater catholicity of taste. In this, as in other realms, most men are provincial in their outlook, and their aesthetic enjoyment and insight are seriously limited by this provincialism. Wise instruction in this field will do much to increase the range of the student's artistic discernments and the catholicity of his artistic preferences. It will help him to see the art he already knows in a new perspective, and it will open up to him wide reaches of artistic achievement of whose very existence he was unaware. He has a right to receive in school whatever formal instruction will promote this wider vision and thus enhance his artistic enjoyment.

(b) *Secondary functions.* The "humanities" have an important secondary function which is analogous to the chief secondary function of the social studies. It is to throw light on the development of the several cultures by setting in relief the artistic and literary expression of this development. The human spirit expresses itself with such sensitivity and precision in art that the study of the art of any period and culture is peculiarly revealing. Art, we have said, can be understood only in historical perspective; but adequate historical comprehension can be achieved only with the aid of the "humanities."

The arts have the additional function of contributing in two distinguishable ways to man's moral discernments. On the one hand, they record with great eloquence and subtlety the artist's interpretation of human life. Morality depends essentially upon a knowledge of how people behave under various circumstances, of what they value and abhor, and of the effects in human experience of various types of emotion, thought, and conduct. The more discerning the artist, the more clearly can he illumine human experience from various perspectives. It is not his task to moralize or to insist with evangelical fervor upon the correctness or perversity of any standards, attitudes, or points of view. Art, at its best, is never explicitly, or even predominantly, propagandistic. What the artist does is rather to put at our disposal that understanding of human nature and human experience which is a prerequisite to wise moral decision. He provides us with the materials for moral evaluation. He makes it possible for us, partly on our own initiative and partly in response to explicit moral and religious instruction, to conceive of moral issues in a concrete and vital human setting, and thus to escape from a type of moralistic abstraction whose inhumanity results in a distortion of moral issues.

The arts also contribute to morality by strengthening and disciplining the imagination which so essentially conditions moral insight. Genuine morality certainly depends in part upon the imaginative identification of oneself with other human beings. The arts are, of course, not unique in their recourse to the imagination or in their power to call it into play. They are pre-eminent, however, in the effectiveness with which they are able to direct the imagination along lines productive of moral sensitivity.

C. *Morality and religion*

The disciplines which concern themselves with morality and religion study man's moral and religious experiences, beliefs, ideals, and practices. Their approach is both historical and systematic. The evolution of moral conventions and ideals and of ethical systems provides material for the systematic consideration of moral beliefs and of the validity of alternative interpretations of moral experience. The origin and development of specific religions are studied with historical rigor, and contrasting religious beliefs and interpretations are examined critically with due regard to their moral implications.

(a) *Primary function.* The primary function of these disciplines in a liberal curriculum is to introduce students to their religious and moral heritage. If they are to be truly educated they must acquaint themselves with what great moral leaders have taught regarding man's nature and his rights and duties. They must also familiarize themselves with teachings of great religious figures and with religious institutions which have been established to preserve and promote them. In short, they must understand as sympathetically and intelligently as possible what men have believed and approved of in the moral and religious realms. The liberal value of these disciplines is evident.

The liberal emphasis on understanding provides the clue to the manner in which these subjects should be taught in a liberal curriculum. It is not the function of the teacher or scholar in any field to engage in propaganda or to evangelize. If propaganda be defined as the dogmatic assertion of a single point of view and the suppression or distortion of other points of view, all propaganda, whether religious or secular, is incompatible with the liberal spirit. And if evangelism be defined as the endeavor to inculcate belief through emotional persuasion, rather than to convince by lucid presentation, evangelism, whether religious or secular, has no place in a lecture room or classroom. Scholars are committed to the open-minded and critical search for truth in all its forms; liberal teachers encourage the student's critical investigation of every academic subject. These standards of objectivity can be adhered to as scrupulously in the teaching of religion and morality as in the teaching of any other subject. A liberal institution will provide its students with appropriate facilities for exploring his moral and religious heritage in this spirit of liberal inquiry.

It is sometimes argued that moral and religious issues are so inextricably bound up with man's emotional nature that they cannot be studied or taught with appropriate objectivity. The danger of losing objectivity must be admitted, but subjectivity and prejudice can be avoided by competent instructors. Morality and religion do not differ in this respect from other controversial subjects, such as politics. There are few issues on which Americans can be more sharply divided than political issues. Does it follow that our schools and colleges should offer no instruction in political theory and practice? The more controversial a subject and the greater man's inclination to decide and act emotionally without knowledge and reflection, the greater the need for factual instruction and for discipline in objective appraisal.

It is also urged that morality and religion are so personal to each individual, so fragile and elusive, that their essence must be lost when they are subjected to historical and critical analysis. The same argument is sometimes used against critical and historical study of the arts; artistic quality also is declared to be so fragile that it cannot survive careful investigation. This sentimental notion is indefensible. All thoughtful students of the arts acknowledge the benefit they have received from their study. There is abundant evidence to support a similar conclusion concerning the study of morality and religion. Distinctive qualities can, of course, be apprehended only through direct acquaintance. To divorce the study of morality and religion from actual moral conduct and religious worship, or to believe that an understanding of what morality and religion really involve can be achieved by mere external observation, without sympathetic insight, would be foolish and uninformed. A liberal study, however, involves no such divorce or belief. Liberal schools and colleges can and should provide moral and religious instruction which will enable students to escape from slavish conventions or complete ignorance, by putting at their disposal relevant facts and by teaching them to interpret these facts in a rational and informed manner.

Actual participation in laboratory experiment, or its equivalent, is essential to a true understanding of scientific inquiry, and ventures in actual artistic creation contribute greatly to the understanding of art. The same can be said for participation in religious worship, since only through such participation can we enter completely into these experiences which yield the empirical data for theological and philosophical interpretation of religion. In many educational institutions opportunity is already being provided for such first-hand experience, whether under official auspices, or through co-operation with local churches and other religious bodies, or through the agency of student chaplains and undergraduate organizations.

That such opportunities should be offered all students who wish to acquire as adequate an understanding of religion as of art or science would seem to be wholly in line with the liberal attitude, which refuses to prejudge any activity or belief. To escape dogmatic provincialism, in this or any other region of human experience, a student must have a first-hand acquaintance with the experience in question. It is essential, however, that the student be given every opportunity to explore conflicting interpretations of religious beliefs and practices, so that here, as elsewhere, he may be free to form his own opinion. The academic, in contrast to the ecclesiastical, justification for providing students with an opportunity to participate in religious worship is that it conditions their academic understanding of this aspect of their tradition and this type of human aspiration. The primary task of a liberal institution is not to train creative artists but to promote the understanding and enjoyment of art. Similarly, the primary task of a liberal institution is not to promote religious conversion but to aid its students in every way to achieve a genuine understanding of religion.

(b) *Secondary function.* The study of morality and religion, like that of the arts, has the important secondary function of complementing the other liberal disciplines. As we have already pointed out, adequate comprehension of any aspect of a culture or of any type of experience involves a knowledge of other aspects of that culture and other types of human activity. The effect of moral and religious ideas and institutions in all periods and cultures has been so far-reaching that no historical understanding of society is possible if this factor is ignored. In our Western culture, for example, the development of the sciences, arts, social institutions, and philosophical systems has been profoundly influenced by moral and religious beliefs. Students who are ignorant of this essential strand in European history are condemned to a highly distorted conception of the other strands in European culture as a whole.

D. *The central role of the humanities*

The humanities, taken together, perform a function which justifies their being given a central place in liberal education in our democratic society. Basic to the American ideal is the belief in the value and dignity of the individual. This belief was exemplified by the earliest settlers, written into our Constitution, and zealously defended by successive generations. Our ideal of freedom is bound up with our ideal of individual integrity, for freedom has significance for us only when conceived as the freedom of individuals. To abandon the right of individual differences is for us tantamount to abandoning freedom. Anything that promotes human individuality, on the other hand, is a truly liberal or liberating agent, and hence of the greatest value to our democracy.

We have seen that morality, religion, and art engage the innermost regions of man's personality. They determine and express his thought, desires, and emotions about what is most valuable in human life. They penetrate beneath mere sensation and ratiocination, mere knowledge of an external world and of social phenomena, to those central experiences of value which condition human individuality and endow human life with meaning. Whoever believes in democracy must believe in the value and dignity of the individual, and whoever believes in this must believe that the disciplines which deepen and personalize human individuality should be allotted a central role in a liberal curriculum.

5. *History and Philosophy*

Since the disciplines thus far considered have all had a distinctive subject matter, we have been able to discuss their nature and their contribution to a liberal curriculum partly in terms of this subject matter. History and philosophy differ in this respect from the other disciplines. Each has its own distinctive problems and methods, and in this sense each may be said to have a subject matter of its own. The primary function of both, however, is to provide integration and synoptic interpretation. So conceived, they have no distinctive subject matter. In their synthesizing role, neither investigates a particular aspect of reality which is not also investigated, within narrower limits and from a more restricted perspective, by one or more of the other disciplines. Their primary task is to relate the specialized activities of the less comprehensive disciplines. Their most significant insights are those which emerge from taking an embracing point of view. Parts acquire new meaning when they are set in a larger context. It is the responsibility of history and philosophy, in combination, to supply this context.

It is this primary function of history and philosophy which we wish particularly to emphasize. But we must first briefly consider the distinctive problems and methods of these disciplines in their more restricted activities. The secondary functions of history and philosophy in a liberal curriculum can best be described in terms of these activities.

(a) *Secondary functions.* We have already referred to the

specialized investigations of history as one of the social disciplines. Here the historian studies various aspects of the past which no other specialists are at present exploring. He is also concerned with problems of historical method; he is continually questioning the nature of historical "fact," "evidence," "interpretation," and "law." Both types of investigation are of intrinsic interest; the past, in all its individuality, is interesting for its own sake, and so are the methods whereby the past can be recovered and understood. From the point of view of a liberal curriculum, these investigations, and the discipline which they afford, are valuable chiefly in making possible the more inclusive and integrative type of historical interpretation.

Philosophy too has its distinctive problems, those, namely, which are dealt with in the specialized studies of logic, epistemology, ontology, axiology, and the like. Philosophers concern themselves also with the historical development of philosophical concepts, methods, and systems. These historical studies not only illumine contemporary philosophical issues by setting them in historical perspective; they also yield insights which are basic to contemporary philosophical thinking. The history of philosophy is an organic part of systematic philosophical inquiry.

These investigations have an intrinsic interest for the philosophically minded, and, in addition, a notable disciplinary value. They provide an exercise in precise and cogent reflection and in the use of powerful abstract concepts. The benefits of this exercise have at least as wide an applicability as have the benefits of mathematical and linguistic study. The student who has explored the thought of a great philosopher with comprehension has thereby acquired a capacity for precise thought and significant interpretation which he can apply to all kinds of problems. The mental processes involved in analyzing anything into its component parts, in relating things systematically, in finding significant likenesses and differences, are similar or identical in all reflection. This is why philosophical discipline, properly conceived, is so admirable a preparation for inclusive and precise thinking in any field.

Yet whatever the intrinsic interest of these philosophical

studies, and whatever their disciplinary value, they too, like the historical studies just considered, merit a place in a liberal curriculum chiefly because they make possible that larger interpretation and integration which is philosophy's primary function.

(b) *Primary function.* The two most significant ways of relating things to one another are the temporal and the systematic. All things are in fact related in time, and all things can be examined with respect to similarities, differences, and basic interrelationships. The historical approach to reality and human experience is primarily oriented to the temporal axis; the philosophical, to the systematic. These two axes, in turn, complement each other, and so do the historical and philosophical approaches. Before considering their mutual dependence, let us note certain characteristics of each.

The historical perspective can, as we have seen, be invoked within any one of the liberal disciplines, since each has its own history. It is important in all of them, since later stages in the development of any discipline can best be understood in their relation to earlier stages. Yet the historical approach is more important in some liberal disciplines than in others.

It is least important in the natural sciences because successive insights in these fields have been for the most part incorporated into a growing organic body of knowledge from which earlier errors have been excluded. The body of scientific knowledge in any generation thus includes, to a notable degree, the funded achievements of earlier generations. Yet there is a growing interest today in the historical development of the sciences, not merely as they constitute strands in an evolving culture, but also as they throw light on the methods and objectives of science as such.

The historical approach is of importance in the social disciplines because their subject matter, human society, is so deeply embedded in and affected by the time process. Social forces and types of social organization can hardly be comprehended if they are abstracted from the historical process in which they have their being.

In the humanistic disciplines the historical approach has unique importance. The moral and religious insights and the artistic achievements of successive centuries, which it is their primary function to preserve and interpret, maintain their value as older scientific and social theories do not. Great moral and religious teachings and great works of art have a timeless and universal character which endows them with significance for all succeeding generations. Hence the study of the past is absolutely essential in all the humanistic disciplines. To ignore the historical development of science and to restrict one's attention to contemporary scientific knowledge is, on the whole, to neglect the chronicle of scientific error without vital loss of scientific insight. But to ignore the history of humanistic endeavor and to attend only to contemporary insights and creations is to cut oneself off from one's humanistic heritage and to condemn oneself to hopeless cultural provincialism.

The historical perspective is thus of greater or less importance within each of the several liberal disciplines. History really comes into its own, however, when these artificially isolated strands are woven together by the historian in the effort to reconstruct a society or culture in its organic unity. The chief duty of the historian is to reassemble what specialists have torn apart and to apprehend the historical process in as concrete a manner as possible. Each of the specialized disciplines, in dealing with its subject matter, traces that strand of history which particularly relates to its own interests. The economist focuses his attention upon the evolution of economic processes and the development of economic theory; the student of the arts studies the development of artistic styles and critical standards. Such selection is necessary and valuable, but it inevitably produces a distortion of the total picture. Society in any given period is a fusion of all these processes, activities, and ideas. The peculiar responsibility of the historian is to reunite these factors and to reconstruct the pattern of any given society in as balanced and rounded a way as possible. Until this integrative task is undertaken, we can have no adequate comprehension of the society in question in all its unity and complexity; and until the several strands of history, economic and political, scientific and artistic, religious and philosophical, are surveyed by the historian in their relation to one another, we cannot hope fully to understand any one of these strands since each was, in the temporal process, so intimately interwoven with the rest.

The philosopher has a comparable task at the level of systematic synthesis and evaluation. He examines the presuppositions, methods, and basic concepts of each of the specialized disciplines and groups of disciplines. These investigations constitute the philosophy of science, of the social disciplines, of art, and of religion. He also examines the relation of art, science, morality, and religion to one another. Only thus can the total character of human experience be apprehended and the interdependence of man's abiding interests be understood. Again, the philosopher applies himself to the problem of knowledge as it arises in each of the liberal disciplines and attempts to clarify the nature of truth and its criteria. He attempts a similar investigation of generic values and of the processes of evaluation. All these inquiries culminate in the metaphysical attempt to give a coherent and reasonable account of reality and of human experience as a whole. Only as this philosophical synthesis is attempted in each successive generation can we hope to combine man's cognitive achievements and acquire that inclusive understanding of our total situation to which each of the specialized disciplines makes an essential but partial contribution.

Though the tasks of the historian and of the philosopher are thus in a sense autonomous, they are, in a more profound sense, not only complementary but mutually dependent. There is a history of philosophy, since philosophical ideas have themselves evolved in time, and there is also a philosophy of history, since the methods, presuppositions, and principles of interpretation invite critical scrutiny. The philosopher cannot afford to divorce himself from historical events; if he does, he exiles himself to a realm of bloodless and meaningless abstractions. The historian cannot afford to ignore those basic interpretative principles which are the philosopher's chief concern, for without these principles history reduces itself to meaningless and unilluminating chronology. If recognition is given to this close interdependence of the historical and philosophical approaches, it is evident that the integrating discipline *par excellence* is historico-philosophical. All significant synthesis is inevitably *both* historical *and* systematic.

The task of historico-philosophical interpretations does not devolve exclusively upon professional philosophers and historians. Their peculiar aptitudes and special disciplines should qualify them to undertake it with unusual competence, and they have the further advantage of being able to devote themselves to it exclusively. Yet every specialist working in a more restricted field must also in his own way, and from the point of view of his own interest, attempt to achieve an historico-philosophical orientation. This is in fact what the more culturally minded specialists are doing at present. They realize the importance of setting specific problems in a larger context in their own field, and of approaching their subject in as historical and philosophical a way as possible. Every specialist must therefore be his own philosopher and his own historian, for only thus can he escape preoccupation with meaningless particularity and apprehend the part in an illuminating context.

The necessity for effective co-operation between professional historians, philosophers, and specialists in the other disciplines is evident. The philosopher and the historian are in continual need of each other's help, and both must draw on the expert knowledge of their colleagues in the more specialized disciplines. The latter, in turn, should be able to go to professional philosophers and historians for assistance in wider orientation—to the historian for a wider historical perspective and to the philosopher for those general concepts in terms of which specialized bodies of knowledge can be effectively related to one another.

History and philosophy, thus broadly conceived and organically related, clearly imply a third axis of integration, namely, the spatial or geographic. The ideal synthesis knows no geographic limitations and transcends the provincial concern with one's own culture at the expense of other cultures, earlier or contemporary. It is natural for man to orient himself first to his immediate geographic environment and to his own culture. A liberal education, however, should help him to discover that his own culture has been influenced by other cultures in other portions of the globe. He thus becomes aware, on the one hand, of the existence of these other cultures and is invited to explore their distinguishing characteristics and their historical development; he becomes aware, on the other hand, of the many factors, geographic, economic, social, political, and religious, which have helped to differentiate one culture from another. Such awareness and the studies which promote it are powerful correctives to geographic, racial, and cultural provincialism and are thus an essential part of a liberal education. Our almost exclusive concern, in formal education, with our own culture and our neglect of the rich and ancient cultures of the Near East and the Far East can only be deplored. The recent growing interest in these cultures and the global thinking which the present war has generated are welcome correctives of this grave limitation. We are learning that our orientation must be world-wide, that an historico-philosophical synthesis is geographic as well, that space is as important an axis of integration as time.

What, then, is the liberal value of such wider synthesis, and what place should it have in a liberal curriculum? This question can best be answered by contrasting the state of provincialism with the ideal of complete cultural orientation. A person is provincial in his thinking if his outlook is restricted, either historically or systematically or geographically. The more marked his myopia, the greater his blindness to other facts or values, other modes of interpretation, other patterns of belief, other "philosophies of life." Such blindness imposes serious restrictions upon freedom of choice, weakens the imagination, frustrates significant reflection, and condemns the victim to a state of opinionated prejudice. This is certainly not the ideal of a liberal education.

A man may be said to be cultured, on the other hand, in proportion to his ability to interpret all the facts at his disposal, all his valued experiences, all his more particular interpretations and beliefs, in an historical, philosophical and global perspective. This ideal is, of course, unattainable, but it can be indefinitely approximated, and the more nearly any individual succeeds in reaching it, the greater his freedom and the richer his experience.

One great desire of young people is to be modern, to see things realistically in terms of present knowledge and present conditions. But most students achieve merely a contemporaneity rather than a genuine modernity of outlook. No one can help being contemporary; but to be truly modern involves the ability to understand and appreciate the distinctive characteristics of the present scene, and to do this the contemporary must be viewed in historical perspective. It is only by studying the present against the background of the past that the full flavor of the present can be apprehended, just as the meaning of the past can be appreciated only by relating it to the present.

Similarly, thoughtful students want to be open-minded, to avoid prejudice and bigotry, to be catholic in their attitude to life and their interpretations of human experience. Yet many of them fail to achieve this objective because of the compartmentalization of their studies and the restriction of their outlook. They learn a good deal about a few things but remain so ignorant of other equally important things that their total perspective is distorted. Education is still conceived primarily as the accumulation of atomistic facts without significant interrelationships. The problem of correcting this situation is one which our academic institutions have only recently begun again to envisage.

It is sometimes urged that this state of affairs is unavoidable, since specialization is essential in each of the liberal disciplines and, by its very nature, precludes wider cultural orientation. The need for some measure of specialization in a liberal curriculum is undeniable, and the difficulty of combining it with a meaningful synthesis is great. But the experiments which are already being conducted in some of our colleges and universities to combine specialization and synthesis indicate that the problem is not insoluble.

It is also argued that the freedom and intellectual integrity of the individual student can be preserved only if he be left to relate things in his own way without guidance or dictation. Teachers, functioning as specialists, it is insisted, should continue to present their students with their specialized contributions, and each student should be obliged to relate and interpret for himself these *disjecta membra*. There is an element of truth in this contention. A student who is familiar with one, and only one, pattern of interpretation is of necessity enslaved to it, and enslavement is inconsistent with the liberal ideal of free inquiry and responsible individual decision. In our desire to escape social and intellectual chaos we must be on our guard against social and intellectual tyranny. There is no reason, however, why such enslavement should take place, for students can be introduced to various types of integration. They need not be offered a neat and complete synthesis of all human knowledge. Such a synthesis, were it possible, would be not only tyrannical but dead and useless. What students need is discipline in the synthetic *method*. They need to learn how to relate things to one another and how to achieve for themselves, with the aid of those who are more experienced and informed, a larger perspective and a more inclusive vision.

Chapter 5. EDUCATION AT THE VARIOUS ACADEMIC LEVELS

PART I

THROUGHOUT the preceding chapters of this report much of the discussion of a liberal education has pointed to the function of that education in freeing the mind and spirit of the individual, and the contribution which such freedom can make to his ultimate happiness—his living "the good life." Some critics have felt that this liberal education has little or no meaning for man in his social relationships and obligations and that the schools supported by the state—especially the elementary and secondary schools—must center their attention upon a "social" program and produce "good citizens."[1] To such critics "liberal education" is satisfactory enough if one can afford it, but it is to be considered a type of education to be obtained only by the aristocratic few *if* and *after* the main business of the public schools has been accomplished for the children of the "common man." We believe, however, that liberal education, as conceived in this report, should be the main business of the public schools throughout the various levels of those schools and that it must be their main contribution to the children of the common man if progress is to be made toward the ideals for which democracy strives.

The "democratic" movement[2] in America has meant, funda-

[1] The following sentence is typical of this attitude. Many others appear in the important educational writings throughout the past twenty-five years.

"Public taxation should not be employed to provide or to train for mere enjoyments that cannot be justified on the basis of positive *social values* to those who pay the bills." (Franklin Bobbitt, *Curriculum-Making in Los Angeles* (1922), 62.)

In general, the effect of the pamphlet entitled *Cardinal Principles of Secondary Education* (1918) has been to emphasize an *ad hoc* training for immediately "useful" results. The common interpretation of these materials has tended toward such a revaluation of the content of primary and secondary education as would (a) stress the contemporary rather than the historical; (b) magnify the importance of social studies; and (c) subordinate the disciplines usually classed as the humanities.

[2] *Democracy* is here conceived as essentially a political concept signify-

79

mentally, that the "common man" has progressively had a larger and larger part in making the decisions that have determined the courses of action of our society. In the past, the chief types of government that we have known have been administered by a narrow ruling class. Comparatively few, and these few selected by the accidents of birth or of wealth, have held the reins of power and have made the decisions for the masses of the people. More and more has this ruling class been broadened until we now have a situation in which the common man has an opportunity to choose and to make his choices effective. It seems clearly our obligation to see to it that the common man, therefore, has the kind of education that will enable him to make enlightened choices and thus justify his place among the ruling class. Only with such an education can he be called "free."

The extent to which a man is free, that is, exercises enlightened choice, depends in the first place upon the extent to which he is aware of the possibilities. In so far as a man is ignorant of what there is to choose, alternatives are eliminated not by rejection but by accident. Freedom is proportional to the range of options. The first condition of freedom, then, is "learning." To promote freedom it is necessary to enlarge the span of man's consciousness by acquainting him both with the world and with "the best that has been known and thought in the world. . . .

That which every man needs to possess in his own right is what will minister to his exercise of choice. I can utilize the enlightenment of others once my choice is made; but I cannot choose by light that does not shine within the chamber of my own consciousness.[3]

In the past, in a society with a narrow ruling class, the common man, who had little or no part in making the decisions that determined the conditions and actions of the society in which he lived, had little *practical use* for an education other than training in the skills of his trade or vocation. To continue now for the common man an education in which vocational skill is predominating,

---

ing the flow of power from the common man—the ordinary citizen. This flow of political power from the common man has within itself the controls that can be brought to bear upon every aspect of our life.

   [3] Ralph Barton Perry, "A Definition of the Humanities," in *The Meaning of the Humanities*, ed. Greene, 1938, pp. 6, 14.

assumes that we still have a narrow ruling class in which the common man has no place and denies all the progress we have made toward the achievement of democracy. We need rather to take the kind of education which formerly was limited to the narrow ruling class, the comparatively few "free" men, and bring it to the much larger body of our citizenry who have become the source of power in our society.

We are concerned, then, chiefly with the education of "free" men in society in which they will have an increasingly greater opportunity to exercise their freedom in the expressing of their decisions upon matters of consequence and in choosing the directions of their social changes. No one, we believe, will argue that the democratic method of social organization is especially efficient, if efficiency is to be measured in terms of quick, short-range accomplishment. Our own practices deny it. Whenever an emergency occurs and the efficient accomplishing of a task is necessary, we dispense with democratic methods of making decisions and adopt those of an autocracy. Military law is declared in the region of an earthquake or a great flood and a single head with almost dictatorial powers is put in charge of arms production in a war emergency. An army under fire would be helpless if it had to adopt the methods of a town meeting. But democratic procedures have their justification primarily in their value as a means of developing the individuals who constitute our society. Democratic organization and liberal education as here conceived go hand in hand. They both rest on the fundamental principle that respect for personality and the maximum development of the individual members of our society is the goal toward which we strive. Training, with little education—an effort to find the particular work which each is to perform and then to provide primarily for the skills needed in this particular work—may be more orderly and "efficient," but it implies a goal fundamentally different from that toward which democracy struggles.

In the discussions of what the schools ought to teach much is said about providing for the "needs" of youth—especially for the needs of those pupils who drop out of school as soon as they have reached the age permitted by our compulsory attendance laws.

But, so far as can be seen, there is no way of determining the "needs" of anybody without assuming some goal toward which we are striving.

It is high time to realize that examining a youngster to ascertain his needs is different from examining him, say, for adenoids. Shall we say, for example, that a pupil with a prominent talent for business needs a commercial course, plus, perhaps a sympathetic acquaintance with our tradition of rugged individualism, or a comprehension of the evils inherent in a system of free competition, or a realizing sense that the love of money is the root of all evil? The answer will not be revealed by any educational microscope. Yet something like this seems to be assumed whenever curriculum making is centered so largely on intensive studies of pupil needs.[4]

From the point of view of this report, then, the goal toward which we strive, and therefore the guide to determining the "needs" of our youth, is human freedom—a freedom of the individual that comes only through understanding, in the kind of society in which the exercise of free choice is not only for the favored few but for the masses of the common people. What has been said in the first part of this chapter concerning the chief emphases of the education that must accompany this freedom will serve as a measure by which to criticize or evaluate some of the significant practices of the schools at each of the various levels.

1. *The Elementary School*

The laws of compulsory school attendance have brought into our elementary schools nearly all the children between the ages of six and fourteen from every class and condition. Among these children there is the greatest range of difference in ability, in home background, and in social outlook. In the mass these children present enormously complex educational problems with which practical educators and school administrators have struggled for a long time. The changes that have occurred in the elementary school curriculum are only in part the result of that struggle.

[4] B. H. Bode, *Progressive Education at the Crossroads* (1938), p. 68.

The elementary-school curriculum has expanded very rapidly during the past century, partly because of the desire of the school to adapt its program to changing social conditions, partly because of the insistent demands of pressure groups in society with special interests. The result is that the curriculum has become disorganized and unwieldy. It consists of many different unrelated subjects.[5]

The elementary schools of the state of New York are required by law to provide instruction in arithmetic, reading, spelling, writing, English language, geography, United States history, civics, hygiene, physical training, the nature of alcoholic drinks, the humane treatment of animals and birds, patriotism and citizenship, highway safety and traffic, fire prevention, and the care and display of the flag. Most of the schools, in addition, teach fine arts, practical arts, music, literature, and science, although instruction in these subjects is not required by law.[6]

It would be unfair to the devoted efforts of a host of schoolmen not to insist here that many of our school administrators and most of our teachers have sought diligently for an effective approach to elementary education, and they have introduced innovations and changed emphases not for the sake of adopting fads as such but because they felt keenly the inadequacy of the old practices and were convinced that there was hope of a remedy in the new. They realized that the memoriter rote learning that once characterized so much of the effort of early school years did not produce satisfactory educational results and they turned away from the "hearing of lessons" to what they called the "teaching of children." The studies of learning had convinced them that "interest" on the part of the pupil was essential, and in their attempts to organize elementary education around "pupil interests" they produced the "child centered" school. But the weaknesses of "child centered" education became apparent in the light of all the social problems made pressing by the distress of the industrial depression and the great numbers of unemployed youth. Educators have more recently tried, therefore, to turn

[5] Leo J. Brueckner and Others, *The Changing Elementary School* (1939), p. 99.
[6] Leo J. Brueckner, *op. cit.*, pp. 100, 101.

the "child centered" school into the "community centered" school with the program centered in the various areas of community activity. The traditional subject matter of elementary education has thus often been crowded into the background to be used or mastered only as the pupil needed it for some purpose of immediate interest.

One needs only a superficial acquaintance with public elementary schools and the problems of the complex situation with which they are struggling to realize something of the tremendous tasks that must be accomplished before the ideals of our society can be realized even in part. In spite of the fact that practically all our children must attend the elementary school, even gross illiteracy still haunts us. Of the 75 million adults in the United States some 3 2/3 million, or nearly 5 per cent, were in 1935 completely illiterate. About half, 34 1/2 million, had not completed the eighth grade. And many, perhaps nearly half our adult population, do not have a reading ability that is sufficient to provide them a basis for thinking independently on many matters of importance.

In spite of the large amount of time which has been devoted to reading in public schools, the net results, even with those adults who have been educated recently, fall short of that maturity of reading ability which is necessary for intellectual independence even in a nonacademic environment. Obviously the independence of thinking which comes from wide reading is beyond the power of large sections of the adult population.[7]

It seems sound to conclude, therefore, that no matter what else is included or omitted, the heart of the elementary school curriculum should be the reading program. All the other activities of the pupil can be made to contribute experience that can be brought to bear upon his reading with comprehension and his reading can be made the means of integrating usefully his whole range of expanding experience. Whether the pupils are to proceed to higher education in the secondary schools or are to leave school as soon as the law permits, their ability to read will determine whether they can grow in the freedom which our type of

[7] Guy T. Buswell, *How Adults Read* (1937), p. 139.

social organization makes possible and upon which it depends for successful operation.

2. *The Secondary School*

The outstanding fact concerning the secondary school in the United States is the tremendous increase in the number of students attending it. In 1900 there were in all types of secondary schools, public and private, approximately 700,000 pupils. Now there are more than 6,500,000. Twenty years ago 28 per cent of our youth between the ages of fourteen and seventeen were in secondary schools; now 63 per cent of this age group attend school. This enormous increase in numbers means, first, that the secondary school pupils now come from a much wider range of social backgrounds than formerly and, second, that the differences in their abilities, interests, and outlook are much greater than ever. It is also frequently pointed out that approximately 80 per cent of those who attend the secondary school do not continue their education in college. It is less frequently noted that two-thirds of this 80 per cent who do not go to college drop out of school before finishing the secondary school, many as soon as they reach the age permitted by the school attendance laws.

The situation indicated by these figures has already furnished the ground for a number of changes in the kind of education provided by the secondary schools and has created strong pressures for still further changes.

(a) There has been much condemning of the materials formerly taught, on the ground that they do not "function" for the mass of high school students in their living. It was perhaps inevitable that school administrators who accepted the educational philosophy of the *Cardinal Principles of Secondary Education* should come to the conclusion that physical education, which was to "function" immediately in better health, and social studies, which must "function" in better citizenship, were of the utmost importance; and that, on the other hand, the study of foreign languages which comparatively few Americans ever "needed to use" was of comparatively minor importance. There has been a growing opposition to all subject matter that could not demonstrably "function" in solving the immediate social problems with which the communities were confronted. The two quotations following are typical of this point of view.

It should be borne in mind . . . that nourishment and sustenance are for life today. Herein lies the suggestion for the control of subject matter. It is to be used for the contribution which it makes to better living in the present. . . . The task for the subject matter specialist is to examine critically the content of his materials in order to discover the elements which are of importance for present living.[8]

With the emphasis primarily upon the past little time can be given to orienting modern boys and girls to the many problems in their own communities, their country, and the present-day world which are so materially affecting their lives. . . . The major function of the modern school thus becomes gaining an understanding of, and successfully dealing with present-day individual and social needs, rather than the passing on of the cultural heritage.[9]

(b) There has been much complaint that the colleges have, by their entrance requirements, dominated the curriculum of the secondary schools and have prevented them from adapting their work to the needs of the great body of students that do not go to college. The attempt of some high schools to separate those students who plan to go to college from those who do not and provide an appropriate curriculum for each group has not furnished a satisfactory solution for this problem. Although the public high schools first found their function in completing elementary education rather than in connecting that education with that of the institutions of higher learning, they gravitated, as did the academies earlier, toward the colleges. There is no doubt that, in the effort to spread the work of a small staff of teachers over both the college preparatory and the general courses, practical considerations lent their aid to the movement toward a program in which college entrance material occupied the central place. There is also no doubt that the college entrance subjects were taught more satisfactorily than were subjects not required

---

[8] "The Development of the High School Curriculum," in The Sixth Yearbook of the Department of Superintendence (1928), pp. 56, 57.

[9] Samuel Everett, "Curriculum Making and the State of the Nation," in The North Central Association Quarterly, Vol. XI (October, 1936).

for entrance and thus tended to supplant the latter by the power of their greater fitness. But the most important factor in the development of the curriculum of the public high schools seems to have been the demand that "since any youth might rise to the highest offices, every youth should have the opportunity offered to him of rising to the highest education," *even if the decision to strive for such an education should not be made until the end of the secondary school course.* Our schools have attempted to avoid blind alleys in education. Wherever differentiated courses have been set up for students not going to college there has been great pressure to make the colleges change their entrance requirements so that such students could be admitted without penalty. Many state universities are now required by law to accept any high school graduate without considering the particular courses of his preparation.

If, then, one recognizes the great diversity of abilities, backgrounds, and interests of the enormous numbers of students now in our secondary schools, and if he accepts the fact that separate courses for the few who will go to college and for the many who will not are not likely to be feasible in many schools, what can be offered as the core of the education our secondary schools should provide?

In spite of all the difficulties we would urge the centering of attention upon an *education* rather than a *training* for both the college preparatory group and the non-college group. We must expect the secondary school to terminate the formal education of those who are to constitute the broad base of our democratic society—of those who are to have more and more voice in determining the direction in which our society is to move. The very fact that most high school students do not continue their formal education beyond this stage obliges us to go as far as we can in developing the enlightenment that will make them "free." In such an education historical perspective is the essential guide to the significance of contemporary phenomena, and a richly developed language experience should help to keep our more able youth from being misled by the malicious verbalisms that cause so much error, waste, and damage in our society. The center of emphasis suggested here must not be taken to mean that other aspects of liberal education can be ignored for our youth between the ages of fourteen and seventeen. Competence and skill for the performance of daily tasks are important, but throughout the secondary school we cannot afford to neglect the fundamentals of the kind of education that is necessary to realize for the "common man" the freedom which is the ideal of our social organization.

3. The Four-Year College

We have become keenly aware of the existence of vigorous criticism of college education, a criticism that has increased since the years of our industrial depression. We have been less aware of the many similar vigorous criticisms that were aimed at college education all through the nineteenth century.[10] In similar fashion we are inclined to view the changes and developments in college education as matters of the last few years, the results of problems newly felt and criticisms recently voiced. It is true that the recent economic and social pressures have had their effects, chiefly in speeding movements started years ago. But to regard the conditions that make the pressing problems of college education as chiefly the result of forces released by the economic disturbances since 1929 is so thoroughly to misunderstand their nature as to make it impossible to evaluate the efforts that have been made to deal with them.

Most striking is the great increase in the number of college students and the consequent change in the character of the

---

[10] The following appeared in a Boston newspaper in June, 1804: "The facility with which the honors of college are obtained induces many to pass through the forms of what is falsely denominated a liberal education, merely for the *name*, and obtaining the *name*, their views are accomplished. Education thus becomes in every sense of the word, too cheap. . . . We must give up the idea of bringing our highest degrees of instruction within the reach of *everyone*, or we must give up the chances of being favored with men of complete erudition. What is lost by bestowing useless and imperfect knowledge on *many*, might well be employed in perfecting the education of the few. . . . The officers of several colleges are aiding the tendency to reformation, by exacting higher qualifications on admission than have of late been required." Quoted from the *Thirty-First Yearbook of the National Society for the Study of Education*, Part II (1932), p. 10.

student body. The increase has not simply brought to the colleges more students with the same kinds of social backgrounds as those who formerly attended college; it has brought the children from an entirely different range of social groups. In England, in France, and in Germany less than 2 per cent of the population between the ages of eighteen and twenty-four have at any time been in the institutions of higher learning; in the United States, 9.2 per cent of the same age group are attending our colleges and universities. Not only is our college student body much less homogeneous than it was formerly, but the chief motives that have brought these masses of students to college are essentially different.

In the United States we have attempted to free the paths of opportunity from artificial restraints and to make it possible for anyone to rise to the highest positions. Inevitably that situation has accented the "struggle to succeed," and "success" has meant chiefly "social advancement." The most effective means of social advancement has been education, and it is probably fair to say that we have this greatly increased proportion of our population in colleges and universities, not because of a genuine desire for learning, but because of the value of education as a tool of social ambition.

Our colleges have taken this enormous mass of students and have tried to accomplish a number of tasks. The machinery used by the colleges for these tasks has changed from time to time and has often been retained after it has ceased to be useful.

(a) The colleges have struggled with the problem of selection. Entrance requirements have not succeeded in keeping out of the colleges those incapable of meeting even the lowest standards of intellectual achievement, and the requirements for graduation, usually expressed in semester credit units, have necessitated no especial intellectual grasp of a large range of subject matter, but chiefly diligence and a memory that would operate reasonably well over a five months' period. The more recent setting up in some colleges of a low hurdle of equivalent "hour points" and "semester hours" at the end of the first two years is another attempt to weed out the unfit.

(b) In the interest of breadth of study, the colleges have attempted to require all students to gain some acquaintance with the major fields of learning. The machinery to accomplish this task earlier took the form of requirements of a certain number of credit hours in each of the several groups of subjects. More recently survey courses in the various fields of knowledge have been instituted.

(c) In order to ensure at least a minimum of intensive study in some particular areas, colleges have adopted the requirements of "majors" and "minors," or so-called subjects of concentration.

(d) In the hope of stimulating interest in intellectual ideals in major and related fields the colleges have used such devices as "honors" courses, comprehensive examinations, reading "periods," tutorial systems, and interdepartmental programs.

The external machinery of college education has tended to become the chief obstacle to a liberal education at this level. Beginning with the device of course credits by which every field is broken up into meaningless units—standardized, interchangeable parts of subject matter based on time exposure—the colleges have sought to deal with all aspects of their problems through prescribed combinations of these units. A normal semester's work results in the accumulation of fifteen credit units. One hundred twenty such credit units have usually been necessary to procure the bachelor's degree. The designers or planners of programs, usually the faculty, have controlled the work of the students by means of the rules for the distribution of these 120 credit units. Typical requirements have been rules such as the following:

The one hundred and twenty hours must include at least twelve hours in each of the following three groups of subjects:

(a) Language and literature.
(b) Laboratory science.
(c) Philosophy and social science.

Students are required to present 6 hours in English composition and 8 hours of foreign language.

Not more than forty hours in one department or eighty hours in a division may be counted toward graduation.

The student must complete not less than thirty hours as prescribed by his department of concentration.

As to quality of work, it is usually required that each of these units be "passed" with a grade of C.

The whole handling of the education of the college student follows closely the pattern of "mass production" in industry. "Mass production" as applied to industry is really more a matter of method than a matter of quantity of output.

As to shop detail, the keyword to mass production is simplicity. Three plain principles underlie it: (a) the planned orderly progression of the commodity through the shop; (b) the delivery of work instead of leaving it to the workman's initiative to find it; (c) an analysis of operations into their constituent parts. . . .

A cardinal principle of mass production is that hard work, in the old physical sense of laborious burden-bearing, is wasteful. The physical load is lifted off men and placed on machines. *The recurrent mental load is shifted from men in production to men in designing.*[11]

Such machinery of college administration may simplify the activities of the teacher but it can thwart the education of the student. It is folly to expect it to create a real sense of the relationships involved in various fields of knowledge, when such relationships are not part of the enthusiasms of the teacher. Academic machinery is harmful in so far as it takes the place of designing and planning by the student, the thoughtful welding together of his activities into an educational coherence.

Although one gains the impression that college faculties as groups discuss little except the machinery that is designed to control the lower levels of student achievement, there are many colleges that have struggled with the complex problems of real education at this level and their programs provide excellent opportunities and intelligent stimulus and guidance. Such a program as that in which the student is asked *in the first two years* to

(a) Gain some coherent understanding of the culture (history, institutions, social and economic conditions, literature, philosophy,

[11] Henry Ford, "Mass Production," in *Encyclopaedia Britannica* (13th ed.), New Vol. II, pp. 822, 823.

etc.) of some period—a time other than that in which the work of concentration is to be done;

(b) Master the rudiments of some one science, with an attempt to understand its aims, its spirit, its methods, and also its place among the sciences and its relation to the general development of science;

(c) Acquire a satisfactory equipment in one foreign language—an equipment that will not only become a tool but will furnish an insight into the nature and function of language as well as some understanding of a foreign people;

and *in the last two years,* with the guidance of small group discussions under competent leadership, to attempt to acquire competence in some one rather broad field of study and understand its bearing upon those areas of knowledge to which it is most closely related—a program such as this certainly gives promise of providing a sound liberal education.

Too often, in the departments of our liberal arts colleges, the courses are now highly professionalized. In most cases even the introductory courses are definitely planned as a first step for those who will make that subject the chief business of their lives. Seldom do departments in their zeal for a particular subject consider the educational bearings of that subject for the mass of students whose contacts with it come from the exploration of interests centered in other fields. These comments must not be construed as a plea for survey courses in each field, courses which attempt to view a whole subject but give the student little concrete experience in it. It is rather a plea that, within each department of our colleges, thought be taken for the demands of a liberal education and that at least some of the work offered be relieved of a strictly professional tone and emphasis.

4. *The Preparation of Teachers*

Although freedom is a condition which must be won by the individual, the efforts of that individual can be greatly aided or greatly hindered by the circumstances in which he is placed. In the schools the most important element for the pupil is the teacher. In the direct contact between the teacher and the student there is the opportunity to make real to him the promised land

and thus to stimulate his efforts to possess it. Here also the student should find that guidance which will keep his efforts from repeating the slow process of trial and error and lead him into paths that will prove fruitful. If the teacher is to be competent to lead and direct the education of his pupils toward winning a larger freedom he must himself first have attained some degree of that freedom. If he is to stimulate their intellectual curiosity he must himself possess the passion for knowing and a sense for the unsettled problems of his field. This implies a liberal education for the prospective teacher.

Those who have been chiefly responsible for the preparing of teachers, however, have felt most keenly the immediate practical needs of the schools and have quite naturally centered their attention first upon the devices of teaching and of school management. Thus professional preparation for teaching came to mean acquiring a knowledge of methods, of class routine and discipline, and developing skill in the mechanics of imparting information. Attainment of the *"art of teaching"* was felt to be the crucial need of teachers. Many teacher-training institutions aimed to initiate the prospective teacher so that, upon beginning his service, "every step should be a repetition, not a venture." The following quotation is typical:

The first and sole consideration in planning a teacher's preparation is the question: Does this feature contribute most to the effective discharge of the particular duty in view, as the welfare of the service requires? Personal considerations are beside the mark.[12]

In application, this principle was at first, and at times is even yet, very narrowly interpreted. In keeping with the changing conceptions of the nature of the teacher's work, however, it has pointed the way from time to time to new emphases in his preparation. At first it led to giving the prospective teacher "review courses" in the subject matter he would be expected to teach. As the emphasis in our educational theory passed from teaching textbooks and "hearing of lessons" to the teaching of "subjects," the meager knowledge of the teacher was felt to be inadequate,

[12] *The Professional Preparation of Teachers,* Bulletin No. 14, Carnegie Foundation for the Advancement of Teaching, p. 11.

and there came the demand for "new-view" rather than "review" courses in order to supply what was termed the "teacher's margin of knowledge." But "the needs of the practitioner in his practice" still determined the amount and the character of these advanced subject matter courses. Many argued and still do argue that advanced knowledge of a subject has little or no direct relation to practical success in teaching that subject either in the elementary or in the secondary schools. Some feel that such advanced study beyond the specific needs of the immediate teaching problems is not only a waste of time but even a handicap.

The demand for more knowledge of the "subject" on the part of the teacher was further restricted by a changed emphasis in educational theory, insisting upon the teaching of "pupils" rather than the teaching of "subjects." From this emphasis has arisen the "need" for the study of psychology and whatever else is deemed necessary to "understand" children. Later came the movement for the "professionalizing of subject matter courses" on the ground that teachers will inevitably not only teach the materials they have been taught in their college courses but also reproduce the methods by which they have been taught. And more recently, with the emphasis upon the "community centered" school, has come the demand that all teachers in order to know the "community" must include in their preparation actual participation in various phases of community activity.

The conflict of view concerning teacher preparation again presents the issue of education against training, and we would press the demand for a liberal education as the first essential of a teacher in an educational system that will serve the ideals of our society. The liberal attitude will lead the prospective teacher out into a broad knowledge not because he arbitrarily sets himself to do some work in many branches of learning, but because knowledge is not really separated into exclusive fields, and to follow up any intellectual problem in its human bearings will necessarily take one through a wide range of subject matter.

The courses which the prospective teacher pursues in attaining this liberal education must be taught and realized in terms of his own mental level. In the college the prospective teacher is attaining his own freedom in his field, is struggling to build up his own point of view and to adjust the new material to his own experience. He should also be sensing the unsolved problems of his subject. Successful college teaching must meet the demands of the college student in his own personal development, and we cannot afford to neglect them for the sake of adopting procedures which can later be imitated in the secondary school. Any attempt to deal with subject matter in terms of the experience of elementary or secondary school pupils or by means of methods applicable to younger (even if keener) minds will tend to thwart the prospective teacher's own progress toward real education.

A part of that education, however, should be the attempt to understand the school as that great institution of society which is devoted to the education of our children. To have thought through the material of his field in terms of educational values and ideals, to have mastered for that purpose a knowledge of the growth of the outstanding theories of education and a familiarity with the conflicting aims now evident in school practices—these are part of the necessary education of the teacher as a leader in the school system. Such matters are the function of the so-called "education" courses.

Finally, the prospective teacher must be sensitized to the mental reactions of pupils. This sensitiveness to what is going on in the minds of pupils, to recognize "the giving of the mind without reserve or qualification to the subject in hand," to understand the signs of its absence—this sensitiveness cannot *be given* to prospective teachers, or lectured or discussed into them, nor attained even in "analyzing their own experiences" in learning or relearning the subject matter they are later to teach. It is won only, if at all, from direct contact with the pupils themselves. Periods of "observation" or "practice teaching" will fail to fulfill this function if they are devoted primarily to "apprenticeship" and developing "teaching technique." From the apprenticeship point of view the attention of the observer or practice teacher is centered upon the activity of the teacher and the acquiring of skill in teaching. But "immediate skill may be got at the cost of the power to go on growing," and if the prospective teacher would develop this sensitiveness to the mental reactions of pupils he must center attention not on what the *teacher* is doing but on what is going on in the minds of the *students*. He must be stimulated not only to seek teaching methods but also to feel keenly the play of mind on mind; he must learn to sense at once when teacher and pupil are not in contact, and the causes of any failure to do so. In so far as this sensitiveness is developed, and only on that condition, is the way prepared for continued growth in teaching.

5. *The Graduate School*

Any helpful consideration of the education furnished by our graduate schools must start with a clear notion of the masses of students now in these schools—their numbers and the purposes that have led them, in many cases, to make great personal sacrifices in order to continue their study.

Complete statistics for all the universities of the country are not at hand but the following figures from thirteen midwestern institutions for the year July 1, 1939, to June 30, 1940, will help to give something of the picture.[13]

> Number of Master's Degrees granted
> July 1, 1939-June 3, 1940......5,294
> Number of Doctor's Degrees granted
> July 1, 1939-June 3, 1940.......1,063
> Number of distinct "departments" in
> which the degrees were granted....145

In the thirteen graduate schools here represented there were, in the summer session of 1939, 20,078 students seeking the master's degree; in the semesters following, 15,458. Although there is no way of knowing what duplication there was in these two totals, it is safe to assume that the number receiving the master's degree was not more than one-fourth of those studying

[13] Compiled by George E. Carrothers, *Number of Students in Thirteen Midwestern Universities and Number of Degrees Granted* (Ann Arbor, 1941).

for it. The number of those who received the doctor's degree was approximately one-fifth of the students enrolled for that degree.

If these thirteen graduate schools can be taken as typical, we can probably trust the following general statements:

(a) The numbers in our graduate schools have increased greatly during the last twenty years. Those seeking the master's degree outnumber those seeking the doctor's degree in the ratio of about four to one.

(b) Comparatively few students for the master's degree receive that degree after but one year of continuous study, for less than one-third of those enrolled as students seeking it during the academic year receive it in that year. Many attempt to qualify for the master's degree through successive summer sessions.

(c) Comparatively few students for the doctor's degree receive that degree after the minimum three years of graduate study. The average time seems to be approximately five years.

(d) Comparatively few graduate students have come directly from their undergraduate study into the graduate school. The average age of those receiving the doctor's degree is about thirty.

(e) The great number of distinct "departments" in which the degrees were conferred in one year seems to be evidence of a somewhat mechanical specialization. It shows at least that the degrees were given in "narrow" formal fields.

Altogether, a realistic view of the graduate school as it is now forces one to conclude that it has become to a large extent—at least in the minds of many of its students—a *training* school for a narrow range of vocations. The great increase in the number of students seeking the master's degree has accompanied the growing practice of many school systems to require that degree as a necessary part of the high school teacher's equipment. And many high school teachers who have been in service seek the graduate study that leads to the master's degree as a means of gaining that increased control over the subject matter of their teaching which experience has shown them to be desirable. Criticisms of the work of the graduate school from this group often reveal the attitudes of the students toward their own study. Because they regard their work for the master's degree as essentially an equipment for high school teaching, they usually express impatience with the required courses that do not seem to be immediately "useful" for that purpose. The greatest number of those who seek the doctor's degree[14] plan to teach in colleges and universities and look upon the procuring of their degree as a necessary step toward a satisfactory position. Here again many of the most vigorous criticisms directed against the particular work required for the doctor's degree assume that the purpose of the course of study is to prepare college and university teachers for their positions and express condemnation of whatever cannot be shown to be directly "useful." It is this attitude on the part of the students that has helped to push a formal or mechanical specialization and has made popular those curricula which aim to train an individual to do a highly specific thing.

Some of the machinery which tends to thwart real education in the college operates also in the graduate school. Here too knowledge is broken up into meaningless units and the students' work is evaluated in hours of credit. The quantity and the quality of the requirements for the master's degree are usually controlled by rules concerning hours of credit in the "department" of specialization. A movement to correct the tendency toward "narrow" specialization shows itself in a growing requirement for some "hours credit" in "cognates." For the doctor's degree, however, the hours of credit play a minor role and the student must demonstrate his control of the field both by examinations and by a piece of research, the results of which are presented in a dissertation.

Severe criticisms of practically every aspect of the work of the graduate school abound in the publications that contain discussions of the education furnished by our institutions of higher learning. The amount of the discussion and the vigor of the criticism have been in some measure an index of our increasing interest and anxiety for the functioning of the "university." We

[14] These are, of course, those seeking degrees in the sciences who aim to become workers in our important research laboratories. These too usually look upon their work for the doctor's degree as specific training for their vocations and their outlook is often narrowly technological rather than deeply and broadly scientific.

cannot in this report attempt to summarize or analyze the various types of these criticisms; we must try simply to point out a few of the conclusions to which we come if we endeavor to measure some of the common features of the work of our graduate schools by the ideal of education maintained in these pages.

As it now stands, most of the work for the master's degree continues the practices of the college, even of the more elementary courses of the college. It assumes the continuing "immaturity" of the students and proceeds accordingly to lay the emphasis on the acquiring of more information and more precise information. We believe that the graduate school should also and especially provide for the weaning of its students from the "authority" of texts and teachers. Some piece of independent work no matter how limited, some attempt to sense the unsolved problems in a field, to see the new problems created by new knowledge, to struggle with some of the firsthand evidence that bears upon some such problems, and to try to grasp a problem in its context, seems to be the only type of experience that will tend to develop in the young graduate student a sense of independence and stimulate the kind of integration that is the burden of this report. With such an emphasis practical considerations will make it impossible to insist on "courses" enough to cover a field or even adequately to "fill in the gaps." But there must be faith that "educated" men can be allowed to do some things for themselves. For the master's degree there should be some consistent program that takes the student to fundamental sources.

The more advanced work of the graduate school, that required for the doctor's degree, cannot fulfill the ideal of education here set forth if it is dominated by a highly professional attitude. Nor should the research which constitutes a major element of the education of the doctor be required to prove its "usefulness." It has served its purpose if it has provided the discipline and insight which should characterize the search for truth and the interpretation of new knowledge and ideas.

Intensive study of phenomena under the most favorable possible conditions—the phenomena of the physical world, of the social world, of the aesthetic world, and the ceaseless struggle to see things in re-

lation—these I conceive to be the most important functions of the
modern university. . . . But the university will not exhaust its function
when it piles up its heaps of knowledge. Within the same institution
that is busy in ascertaining facts, intelligence will be at work piecing
facts together, inferring, speculating. . . . It is fashionable to rail at
specialization; but the truth is that specialization has brought us to
the point we have reached, and more highly specialized intelligence
will alone carry us further. But, of course, specialization alone does
not suffice; there must somehow be drawn into the university also
minds that can both specialize and generalize. The philosophic
intelligence must be at work trying new patterns, trying, however
vainly, to see things in the large, as new material is accumulated.[15]

Perhaps the most important need of our graduate schools is
more active academic leadership, minds that are critical but not
pedantic, that are enthusiastic in the search for truth and given
not only to the conservation of knowledge but especially to its
interpretation. Too often the heads of such schools become devoted to the machinery of organization and administration—
machinery which thus takes on a factitious importance and inter-
feres with, if it does not thwart the full realization of the best
that our highest education could produce.

Throughout all the levels of our schools "faith in machinery
is our besetting sin." The pressure to get things done leads us to
a materialistic practicality that stresses vocationalism rather than
education. We constantly seek some magic short cut in education,
some way to quick and easy accomplishment; we are deceived by
quack educational devices as by quack medicine. We are not
patient enough to take the long view and wait for the processes
of liberal education to work. The attainment of freedom will be
slow but faith in its realization is fundamental in the ideals
toward which democracy strives.

PART II

The role of liberal education at the various academic levels
has been discussed in Part I of this chapter with particular
reference to existing educational trends in the humanities. We

[15] Abraham Flexner, *Universities: American, English, German* (1930),
pp. 23, 24.

shall now summarize as affirmatively as possible the full implications, for each of the academic levels, of our earlier analysis of
liberal education in a democracy. It was our contention that a
liberal education is not only uniquely qualified to prepare man
for the good life, but that it is the only effective preparation for
responsible citizenship and, at the same time, the necessary basis
for, and complement to, vocational and professional training. If
this contention is valid, liberal education should be assigned
priority throughout the educational process, though this emphasis must not be allowed to obscure the importance of specialized forms of training.

1. *Objectives and Conditions of Liberal Education*

In analyzing the nature and function of liberal education at
the several academic levels we must keep in mind the following
considerations:

(a) A major weakness of formal education today is its tendency toward too narrow specialization. Particularly are our abler
students being permitted, and often encouraged, to study a
limited subject matter from a limited approach, at the expense
of other subjects. On the other hand, what is frequently called
"general education" is often superficial. Witness the attempt to
introduce students with no preliminary training to the whole
field of art and literature, the social studies, or the natural
sciences, in one brief elementary course, or the attempt to
"cover" the whole of history or to "survey" the whole of philosophy in a quick and easy gallop. Here depth is so completely
sacrificed to breadth that the student cannot be expected to
achieve any genuine understanding of the questions at issue
or to escape bewilderment, growing distaste, and finally boredom.
The task of the liberal educator must be to steer between narrow
specialization and superficiality.

(b) Students have certain basic needs which demand satisfaction; but they also manifest widely different types of interest
and aptitude. Some are more theoretically, some more practically
minded; some have a greater aptitude for intellectual analysis,
some for artistic and other forms of creation; some exhibit a

natural leaning to the more mathematical and scientific disciplines, some for humanistic studies, and some for social problems; some are by temperament narrow specialists and some are more philosophically and historically minded. Students differ also in natural ability and learning aptitude. We may be in some danger of favoring the abler student at the expense of the less able; we are certainly in far greater danger of penalizing the abler student by holding him back or by failing to encourage him to advance as rapidly as his native ability would permit. Here we see false democracy at its worst, namely, as tending to reduce all men to one dead level, stifling initiative and frustrating potential leadership.

The corrective for this weakness in our educational system is allegiance to the ideal of our democratic society, which claims for every young person the right to the kind and the degree of education which he is qualified to assimilate. This safeguards the rights and needs of less able students, but it also provides for the education of abler students. To suppose that the democratic ideal necessitates a denial of varying aptitudes or a willful suppression of special talent is preposterous, and to fail to recognize such talent and to foster it is suicidal. One of our greatest needs today is for competent leadership. Leaders cannot be produced in any field of human activity unless those young people who have the capacity for leadership are given all possible assistance to develop their aptitudes and make their richest contribution. It is therefore important that those in charge of educational programs, at whatever level, should so far as possible differentiate between not only various types of students but students of different degrees of ability.

(c) Teachers and administrators must somehow hit a happy mean, in their handling of students, between educational regimentation and educational anarchy. In a totalitarian state prescription is the rule, and what is thus prescribed is taught in the spirit of dogmatic indoctrination. In our democratic society the spirit of intellectual *laissez faire* has become increasingly dominant; we have been so afraid of academic prescription that we have encouraged academic license. This refusal to provide our students with the academic guidance to which they, as young people, are entitled, and which we, as their academic elders, are under obligation to offer, has resulted in much academic, cultural, and social confusion. Unless teachers and administrators are wise enough to provide students with the guidance and instruction which they should receive at each educational level in preparation for higher levels, and for intelligent living and responsible citizenship, we might as well abandon the pretense of academic instruction altogether and invite our young people to acquire an education as best they can in public libraries. It is our business to be wiser in these matters than our students can possibly be. We should insist that at each stage of the educational process they should study those subjects which experience has shown to be essential steps toward freedom.

With these broad considerations in mind we can now proceed to consider more specifically the ideal pattern of education at each of the main academic levels.

2. The Elementary School

Discrimination between students at the elementary school level should, for the most part, take the form not of penalizing the less able students but of encouraging and stimulating the abler ones.

The responsibility of the elementary school to its abler students is to provide effective instruction in those basic disciplines which must be mastered in preparation for successful study in high school. These disciplines include reading, writing, arithmetic, geography, and the like. The importance of such instruction is evident in view of the tendency, particularly in certain types of elementary schools, to neglect it. These subjects can, of course, be taught in so mechanical and unimaginative a manner that the children are made to hate their studies and to derive little benefit from them. They can also be taught in so superficial and sentimental a manner that the children fail completely to learn those basic facts without which no significant progress is possible. The competent teacher will avoid these opposite dangers, and the child fortunate enough to be under such a teacher will acquire with relative ease and genuine satisfaction proficiency in these important basic disciplines. He will be able to proceed to high school without the tragic handicap of an undisciplined and unfurnished mind or, alternatively, of a deeply rooted aversion to all rigorous study.

It is also the task of the elementary school to stimulate the student's interest and to help him to achieve some preliminary integration of his knowledge and interests. Even a young child can be helped to appreciate the significance of isolated facts by having them set in a wider context, and he can be induced to study various subjects with greater enthusiasm if the relevance of such study to his daily life is made apparent. But the elementary school teacher must be on guard against confusing momentary excitement with sustained and growing interest. It is easy to arouse a child's superficial interest by introducing him prematurely to issues whose true significance he is not yet able to grasp, and, in the process, to spoil his appetite for these issues at a later stage. However great the importance of integration at every stage of education, it is bad pedagogy to force upon a child a pattern of integration which is beyond his grasp; if this is done, this same pattern must fail, when the child is more mature, to awaken that interest which it would awaken were it presented then for the first time. The elementary school teacher must beware of "skimming the cream" and of thus precluding the possibility of arousing and holding the student's interest when he is older.

The elementary school should also keep in mind the great educational importance of appropriate manual training and instruction in the creative arts. If such training is regimented and made compulsory, children without aptitude along these lines will be made miserable and will acquire a lasting distaste not only for such activity but for its concrete products. But there can be no question that such instruction can provide many children with a most valuable type of discipline, that it can teach them a useful manual dexterity, and that it can be made to strengthen and fructify whatever creative capacity they may possess. Here the danger to be avoided is overemphasis at the expense of the more academic disciplines.

The elementary school should thus provide the basis for liberal education at the higher educational levels for students who are destined to enter high school. It can do so by equipping them with the tools and the habits of mind which they will need later. These can be acquired in early youth; children can learn to read and master the rudiments of mathematics at the elementary school ages. One of the tragedies of American education today is the failure of so many children to acquire this linguistic and mathematical equipment at the appropriate time.

The elementary school must also give those children not destined for high school as much of a liberal education as possible. Only thus can they be prepared to assume the responsibilities of citizenship and to lead rich and satisfying lives. It may be necessary to devise a somewhat different program through elementary school for students of this type. But, by and large, the type of education best adapted to the student headed for high school is identical with that which would most benefit those who will never reach high school. The latter need as rigorous a discipline in reading, writing, arithmetic, and so forth, as their more fortunate fellow students. Whatever early differentiation between abler and less able students is possible at this stage would therefore seem to dictate not radically different programs but adequate provision for the more rapid advancement of the abler students, patient and skillful instruction of the less able.

3. High School and Preparatory School

At the high school level the need for wise differentiation between the abler and less able students is intensified. There are some students in every high school whose capacity for more advanced instruction along academic lines is in no doubt, and provision should be made to give these students a sound preparation for college work. This instruction should be predominantly liberal in character, with continued emphasis on mathematics and language study and with courses in science, history, the arts and literatures. The tendency today of many high schools to ignore the future educational needs of their abler students is deplorable.

The task of the high school is, however, a multiple one, since only a minority of its students are destined for college. No system of differentiation of purely academic aptitude can satisfactorily separate those for whom education in the high school must be terminal from those for whom it is preparatory. It is often impossible for the authorities to determine during the high school course how much ability for college work each individual student actually possesses, since a student who shows little promise at a given age may develop great promise later. Neither can the authorities know in advance what the financial resources of their students will be at the end of their high school course.

There seems to be only one practical solution, namely, to provide all students at this level with as complete a liberal education as each can assimilate. In this way the danger of premature differentiation is obviated, and no child is condemned by well-intentioned teachers to a more restricted program than his true ability warrants. Such a policy will also prove advantageous in the long run to those students who never reach college. The studies which will prove most useful to those who do enter college are equally useful to those who do not. Only with the aid of these disciplines can the latter hope to pursue their education on their own initiative after leaving high school. Our tendency to assume that education must cease with the termination of formal academic instruction betrays a shocking lack of confidence in our ability to cultivate in our students interests and habits of thought which will prompt them to further education on their own momentum. The increasing popularity of courses in adult education testifies to the desire of the academically underprivileged for more education, and this group is entitled to receive, during its high school years, the best possible foundation for the liberal pursuit of learning.

4. *The Four-Year College Course*

The main objective of a four-year course should be to provide the student with the opportunity to continue his formal liberal education. The following conditions must be satisfied if this objective is to be realized:

(a) Provision should be made for preliminary orientation in the main liberal disciplines. Only thus can the student be introduced to the educational possibilities which are open to him and to the basic relationships between these disciplines. The complexity of the subjects in question, the frequent need for more or less specialized instruction as a prerequisite to the understanding of their nature and significance, and above all, the specialized approach of most college professors, make the provision of such initial orientation difficult. Yet, until this problem is solved college students must continue to fumble their way through college without orientation or intelligent purpose and with intellectual confusion.

The need for such orientation is intensified by the unevenness and inadequacy of the students' prior education. They come to college from schools with different educational programs, standards, and conceptions of the academic disciplines. If these students are to work together effectively for four years, they must acquire some common background and common tools.

(b) The college student should also have relatively intensive instruction in some one of the major disciplines or groups of disciplines. Only thus can he learn what it means to investigate any subject with rigor and adequacy. In emphasizing wider integration we must not sacrifice the benefits of intensive and specialized study.

Much depends upon the way in which such specialized studies are directed. The field of concentration may be unduly narrow and isolated from other major fields; it may be so immense as to preclude the possibility of mastering basic methods and concepts in the time available. Learning of isolated facts and methodology may also be insisted on at the expense of illuminating interpretation. It is therefore important to define major fields of specialization wisely and to supervise with care the manner in which these fields are explored.

(c) Provision should be made for as complete an integration of all the work done in college in the several fields of study, major and minor, as is possible. Here the following considerations are relevant: First, the earlier the student is compelled to complete his integrative survey, the less rich and mature is such integration likely to be. Ideally, the student should progress toward a culminating integration at the end of his senior year; he should be helped to pull together, so far as possible, all that he has learned during his four-year course. Second, the narrower the field of major concentration, the more important is it that he should acquaint himself as widely as possible with other major disciplines. Third, the narrower and the more technical the individual courses offered in the college program to students not majoring in the field in question, the more difficult must they find it to elect courses which will contribute effectively to their liberal education. The present organization of courses constitutes a major academic problem today. Courses are usually devised as steps on a ladder leading to intensive specialization in the given field. As a result, they frequently have little value for students who are not prepared to ascend the entire ladder, rung by rung. More effective ways must be devised for meeting the needs of those students who will not major in a given field and who will have only a limited amount of time to devote to this field. This may involve the introduction of new courses explicitly designed for these students or, alternatively, the creation of introductory courses which will provide requisite instruction both for those who major in this field and those who do not.

(d) The principle of differentiation is as applicable at the college as at the high school and elementary school levels. Abler and more ambitious students should, especially during their last two or three years in college, receive the type of instruction best adapted to their special needs and aptitudes. If they are forced to go the pace of less able students, they are bound to lose interest and thus fail to make the progress they might otherwise make.

But the principle of differentiation need not carry with it the implication that students headed for specific vocations and professions after leaving college should, on that account, undertake radically different programs of study. Certain basic prerequisites for admission to graduate schools must, of course, be satisfied, and certain other courses may contribute directly to vocational proficiency. But all college students should be urged to devote as much as possible of their college course to the acquiring of a liberal education, whatever their plans for the future. If they are headed for a vocation which can engage only a few of their aptitudes and interests, they will need, for their vocational success, precisely that discipline which a liberal education is able to provide. In short, all students who are able to complete a four-year college course should be advised to devote their four years to a liberal program as the best possible preparation for life and, indirectly or directly, for whatever vocation or profession they may enter.

5. *Vocational and Professional Training*

It is impossible to draw an absolute line between vocational and professional training; they differ not in kind but in degree. Yet, for practical purposes, that type of training can be entitled "vocational" which consists in the acquisition of techniques requiring somewhat less general thought and imagination, and which presupposes relatively little liberal education. That type of training, in contrast, which makes more extensive demands upon the individual's intellectual and imaginative powers, and which therefore presupposes more liberal education, can be entitled "professional" training. Both vocational and professional training must be assigned an important place in our educational system.

(a) *Vocational training.*

(i) Students should be urged to start their vocational training as late as possible and to get as much liberal education as their abilities and economic resources permit. They should be so advised both for economic and for cultural reasons. The strictly economic value of a liberal education is becoming more evident even in the vocations. The more education of this type an individual has received, the greater is his ability to adapt himself to changing conditions, technical innovations, and novel problems, the greater is his social prestige among his vocational associates and in his community, and therefore the greater the economic rewards for which he may reasonably hope. The intrinsic value of liberal studies to the individual himself should be evident; the more restricted and mechanical his vocational activity, the greater will be his need for a liberal education as preparation for an intelligent and fruitful use of leisure and as a general humanizing influence.

(ii) Vocational training should give due recognition to any intrinsic satisfactions which the specialized activities in question may occasion. Perfect functional utility may itself be a source of intrinsic delight and this delight will enhance the total satisfaction to be derived from activities whose primary function is utilitarian. Notable skill in any field possesses a value comparable to the value of "elegance" in pure mathematics and merits cultivation even though it is secondary to what is here the primary value, that is, efficacy in achieving practical objectives.

(iii) Vocational programs should not be allowed to impair the scope and efficiency of liberal programs. It is natural for schools and even colleges, in their enthusiasm for vocational programs, to permit liberal studies to be crowded to the wall. The result of such a policy is bound to be disastrous in the long run.

Institutions with strong liberal programs have tended to divorce themselves completely from all vocational training. This has its disadvantages. On the one hand, vocational programs and those concerned with them, both as teachers and as students, suffer from such a divorce by being deprived of contact with more liberal and cultural endeavor, and those engaged in liberal academic pursuits lose the benefit of contact with more immediately practical activity. Both types of activity can benefit from wise association; a liberal atmosphere can humanize vocational studies, and vocational pursuits can orient liberal studies to the more immediately practical necessities of human life.

(b) *Professional training.* Professional training is of three main types: first, training for non-academic professions, such as law, medicine, journalism, commerce, and business administration; second, training for scholarly research and for academic instruc-

tion at the college and graduate levels; and third, training of high
school and elementary school teachers.

(i) Specialized training for the non-academic professions presupposes considerable liberal education, and the more "learned"
the profession and the higher the standards of the professional
school, the greater the need for a cultural foundation and orientation. Recognition of the professional value of a liberal education
is at present increasing rather than decreasing. Those in charge
of professional schools are discovering by experience that those
students who have received a sound liberal education are not only
better equipped for effective work in graduate school but are also
more likely to be successful in their profession in later years.
Recognition of this fact is evidenced by the disposition of certain
medical schools and law schools to lessen rather than increase
their technical entrance requirements and to encourage college
students who propose to apply for admission to graduate school
not to specialize too intensively, while in college, in those subjects
closely related to their future professional activities. Thus, pre-
medical students are being advised not to overemphasize their
work in science, and pre-law students, their work in politics during their college years, but to attempt, rather, to acquire in college
as rich, varied, and rounded a liberal education as time permits.

This tendency should be encouraged, for it is important that
our young doctors, lawyers, journalists, and businessmen should
learn to see their professional activities in cultural perspective
and be able to relate them to enduring human ends and abiding
human interests. Success in these professions depends not only
on a high degree of technical proficiency and specialized knowledge but also on the ability to put technical knowledge to use
in a wise and humane manner. The professions will renounce
their birthright and weaken their potential contribution to society
if they permit themselves to become too narrowly specialized.

Most professional schools still assume that colleges and universities are providing their students with the requisite liberal
background during their undergraduate years. Unfortunately,
many students are going to professional school largely unequipped
to set their professional studies in a liberal and cultural perspec-

tive. The ultimate solution must be left to the colleges and universities; it is their duty to make good their present deficiency. But until they give evidence of having progressed further, professional schools should attempt to offer their students, at the graduate level, something of what they have missed in college.

This problem indicates once again the need for more effective co-operation between various academic levels of instruction. Just as high schools are largely dependent upon elementary schools, and colleges and universities upon high schools and preparatory schools, so too are professional schools dependent upon the four-year college course. Inefficiency and maladjustment at an earlier stage result in inefficiency and maladjustment at a later stage. Continuity in the educational process is the great desideratum, and this can be achieved only through genuine co-operation between the several academic levels.

(ii) Potential scholars and teachers of advanced standing must continue to be trained in the techniques of scholarly research, but this type of training hardly needs emphasis today in view of the predominant attention accorded to it in our graduate schools. What should be emphasized is the need for more liberal orientation and integration at the graduate level of instruction. Narrow specialization is nowhere more evident than here. Our graduate students are not only not being assisted to achieve such orientation in graduate school, but are often actually prevented from acquiring it on their own initiative by an over-insistence on highly technical studies. Our graduate schools are, as a result, modern Towers of Babel. Graduate students live in different worlds, talk different languages, and find it all but impossible to establish intellectual contact with one another. Some administrators have hoped to correct this situation by having students live and eat together, in the hope that this would suffice to establish contact between students in different fields. This hope is largely illusory. It is only in rare instances that graduate students with such different backgrounds, and so deeply involved in different types of investigation, learn to talk a common language, to face common problems, and to give each other the benefit of their respective specialized achievements. Methods must be devised to enable graduate students to make up for the deficiency of their undergraduate courses and to learn how to envisage their specialized tasks from a more synoptic point of view. Until this is done, we must expect these students to become narrow compartmentalized teachers and scholars and to see the liberal disciplines grow weaker. A few graduate schools are at present facing this problem and conducting experiments which may prove fruitful.

(iii) Responsibility for the training of high school and elementary school teachers is at present assumed by teachers' colleges and by the departments of education in various colleges and universities. The nature and objectives of such training can best be discussed with specific reference to teachers' colleges.

These colleges have multiplied rapidly and have achieved great influence in the educational world. Beginning as two-year normal schools dedicated to the training of elementary school teachers, many of them have developed into four-year colleges, and some offer graduate work. In response to the need for large numbers of elementary and high school teachers, these colleges naturally first emphasized pedagogical methods. Their task was to take men and women without special capacity for teaching and train them rapidly to function as teachers. Hence their preoccupation with pedagogical devices, with tricks of the trade, with short cuts and substitutes for genuine education. Teachers largely uneducated in any particular subject have thus been given responsible teaching positions and been compelled to rely on standardized methods of instruction as a substitute for genuine knowledge and genuine teaching ability.

The better teachers' colleges are increasingly aware that successful teaching, quite as much at the elementary and high school levels as at the higher levels, depends upon a mastery of the subject matter to be taught, and that, particularly at these lower levels where teachers so frequently teach more than one subject and where specialization is not required, cultural orientation is at a premium. This trend toward liberal education is salutary and deserves support. But the fact remains that many teachers' colleges are at present ill equipped to provide their students with that type of liberal education which they now seek to offer. The faculties of some teachers' colleges are composed of individuals with less scholarly achievement and less cultural background than are the members of college and university faculties. This relative deficiency is often intensified by a lack of adequate library and laboratory equipment and by a relatively low salary scale. In addition, the old enthusiasm for pedagogy in the narrow, mechanical sense has not completely died out; it is still strong in certain teachers' colleges.

Much can be done to improve the quality and character of the teaching at teachers' colleges through co-operation between them and liberal arts colleges and universities. At present, such co-operation is largely lacking. Colleges and universities are partly responsible for this state of affairs, and in so far as this is the case it lies with them to correct the situation by taking active steps to help individuals and groups in these colleges to improve the quality and pattern of their teaching. Certain universities can also help to correct the present situation by making their departments of education models of liberal instruction and, in addition, by offering summer programs which make available to elementary school and high school teachers the type of advanced training which would most aid their actual teaching.

Chapter 6. CONCLUSION

WE CAN now summarize some of the main conclusions of this analysis by reformulating, in general terms, our most pressing educational needs. We can then recapitulate the salient aspects of an ideal liberal curriculum.

Our greatest weakness today is our lack of genuine culture. This deficiency manifests itself in the superficiality of many of our standards, the poverty of many of our individual experiences, and the inadequacy of our social consciousness. It can be corrected only through liberal education. We are urgently in need of liberally minded and well-educated teachers in charge of programs of study which offer students a sound liberal education as a preparation for responsible citizenship and human living.

Our second great need is for various types of wise differentiation. It is important that each of our institutions, whether tax supported or privately endowed, and of whatever academic level or type, should cherish its own distinctive traditions and character and work out its educational salvation in its own way. Our educational institutions have certain common weaknesses and stand in need of certain common correctives. But this does not preclude the possibility or desirability of each institution's advancing toward a common goal in terms of its own distinctive temper and genius. Mechanical imitation by one institution of another can yield only mechanical and therefore educationally harmful results.

The need for sharper differentiation is evident also within individual educational institutions. We must distinguish more clearly between purely liberal programs and programs which are partly or wholly vocational, between alternative liberal programs, between more and less advanced programs. The interesting experiments now being conducted in various institutions that are offering honors programs or their equivalent are notable steps in the right direction.

We need to differentiate, moreover, between intensive specialization, whether vocational and professional or academic, and cultural orientation. If we fail to do so we are certain to forget the educational necessity for *both* depth and breadth, technical proficiency *and* cultural synthesis, specialized knowledge *and* synoptic vision.

It is absurd to suppose that differentiation is undemocratic, for democracy has never meant, and never can mean, blank homogeneity and absence of variety. It is absurd to call the giving of special educational opportunities to more able students undemocratic, provided that all students with the requisite ability may avail themselves of these opportunities. Democracy demands adequate provision—economic, academic, and social—for the education of its abler citizens.

The need for differentiation is balanced by a need for more effective co-operation. We need co-operation between those in charge of education at the various levels, since no level is in fact autonomous. Since education is essentially a continuous process, we must resist any tendency of elementary schools to ignore the prerequisites of effective work in high school, and of high schools to proclaim their autonomy and insist that colleges and universities accept their students, however ill equipped, for college and university work. Nowhere is the need for co-operative effort more urgent than here.

No institution can succeed in working out integrated programs of study without extensive co-operation between the administration and the several departmental and divisional groups. Business meetings devoted to the machinery of class instruction, teaching hours, and graduation requirements will not achieve the intellectual co-operation which arises from a real interchange of ideas, an exploration of common intellectual problems, a sympathetic meeting of minds. It is discouraging to think how rarely administrative heads find the time or inclination to discuss with the teaching staff questions of major academic importance, and how infrequently faculty members of different departments meet on an intellectual basis. The hope for the future rests chiefly with the younger members of our faculties who have not yet settled into academic grooves. Some of these younger men are at present expressing a healthy dissatisfaction with excessive academic departmentalization. We must turn to them, to some of their older colleagues, and to the enlightened college administrator, for initiative and guidance in the task of constructing and operating integrated programs of study.

The possibility of achieving educational reforms, at whatever level and in whatever type of institution, will depend upon the clarity with which those who are attempting to initiate these reforms are able to distinguish between ultimate and immediate ends, basic and subsidiary values, and their relation to one another. The wisdom required includes recognition of the conceptual tools and the habits of mind, as well as the physical instruments, such as laboratories and libraries, which are essential to a liberal education; of factual knowledge, memory, and instruction in research and critical inquiry; of aesthetic, moral, and religious sensitivity; of specialization and integration; of a capacity for reflective commitment and responsible action. Only as we realize that a liberal education is a difficult achievement requiring much of the individual, and making it necessary that he receive abundant and expert help, can we hope gradually to approximate the cultural ideal. The prior importance of liberal education must be recognized, but the necessity for vocational and professional training must also receive recognition. These two complementary types of instruction must be wisely balanced to ensure the effectiveness of each. Finally, a central role must be assigned to the humanistic disciplines, since they illumine human ends, but this emphasis must be complemented by the other disciplines with their unique contributions.

Another great need is for wiser and more assured leadership. Since education is itself a specialized activity, educational problems can be envisaged, and solutions for them devised, only by those who are qualified by temperament and education to understand the basic educational issues. Only the scholar can truly comprehend the value and conditions of scholarship, and only the teacher can appreciate the factors upon which effective teaching depends. Teachers and scholars must justify their claim to special competence by offering assured leadership in the field of liberal education, where the shortage of assured leadership is most serious. Many humanistic faculties have lost their way and have forfeited public confidence. Academic "humanists" must reorient themselves, clarify their objectives, and provide the academic community with guidance which reflects a fuller comprehension of basic issues. Our colleges and universities may thus recapture the respect and confidence of high school and elementary school leaders and help to promote, at these levels, urgently needed reforms.

The more clearly faculties and administrations at the several academic levels realize what they are about and what is worth insisting on, the more easily will they be able to determine what measure of freedom and what types of control are most advantageous to their students. The academic *laissez-faire* attitude reflects a confused philosophy of education and a failure to appreciate the nature and conditions of liberal instruction. If we understood the conditions of genuine freedom we could direct our students with assurance and help prevent them from squandering their time and energy in misdirected efforts. The alternative to *laissez faire* is neither regimentation nor indoctrination. It is enlightened leadership which respects the individual student's aptitudes and interests but insists on the mastery of basic disciplines without which he cannot possibly achieve the ends which his own temperament and enduring interests dictate. We must combine discipline and guidance; we must encourage the mastery of means for the realization of desired ends. This is not a policy of compromise. It is the positive principle of finding out what, human nature being what it is and individual variations being what they are, the individual student *really* needs and wants, and of then insisting that the student receive that education which alone can lead him toward his goal.

The complexity and diversity of our educational institutions today make it impossible to recommend specific proposals for curricular changes which would be equally applicable to all institutions, even at the same academic level. Even if it were possible to draft such proposals, recommendations of this type would be incompatible with the ideal of a liberal education in a democratic society. For in such a society efforts to approximate the ideal must be self-initiated and self-directed. Each institution, because of its distinctive traditions, obligations, and opportunities, is in many respects unique. Each institution must therefore develop its own specific educational objectives, appraise its present performance in the light of these objectives, and devise ways and means of advancing more rapidly and efficiently toward its educational goal. It is not the purpose of this report to promote standardization or regimentation in American education.

We have, however, indicated the general principles on the basis of which a liberal curriculum should, in our opinion, be constructed. These principles can be recapitulated as follows:

(a) *Mastery of the basic instruments*. All students, with due recognition of their varying aptitudes, will be helped to master the basic instruments of liberal inquiry. They will receive this instruction as early as possible, partly because at least some of these aptitudes and skills can best be acquired during the formative years, partly because their mastery is a pre-requisite to more advanced study.

(b) *Scope*. An ideal curriculum will include all the major liberal arts and sciences discussed in Chapter IV. Whether or not it is organized according to divisions, it will introduce the student to each of the major disciplines, so that no essential aspect of his cultural heritage is neglected.

(c) *Specialization*. The college and university student will be introduced to the nature of intensive study and scholarly investigation. We must not forget the value of specialized study even for the average undergraduate, especially today when rapid surveys of complicated subjects invite superficial treatment.

(d) *Integration*. The greatest possible integration will be provided between the several liberal arts and sciences. This integration will be both historical and systematic.

(e) *Latitude*. Adequate provision will be made for the student's individual interests and needs. Without abandoning the principle of a balanced academic diet, every effort will be made to give the student appropriate latitude of choice, that is, to enable him to do more intensive work in some fields than in other fields.

(f) *Continuity.* An ideal liberal education will be free from violent discontinuities or sharp breaks in the educational process; it will anticipate at each lower level the academic requirements of the higher levels, and integrate at each higher level what has been achieved at the lower levels.

Our central thesis can perhaps be stated most briefly and dramatically in negative terms. Would we not all agree that a person was *not* liberally educated who was illiterate and inarticulate, uninformed and with no knowledge of how to acquire knowledge, insensitive to aesthetic, moral, and religious values, provincial, unintegrated, and enslaved? Does it not follow, then, that a person *is* liberally educated in proportion as he is literate and articulate in the "languages" of human intercourse, verbal, symbolic, and expressive; as he is possessed of the basic facts concerning the world of nature, human nature, and human society, and, in addition, a master of the main techniques of acquiring new knowledge in these realms; as his native sensitivity to values is cultivated and as he is capable of reflective commitment in the realms of aesthetic, moral, and religious value; as he is freed from the tyranny of provincialism through temporal, spatial, and systematic orientation—in short, as he is an intelligent and responsible agent, able to participate richly in the good life, and ready and eager to contribute all he can to the welfare of his fellow men? Is not this the positive freedom which democracy should cherish and which a liberal education should foster? And is it not our duty and privilege, as citizens, as scholars and teachers, and as human beings, to make liberal education in this country a powerful instrument for human freedom, a bulwark of human dignity, a source of human value?

BIBLIOGRAPHY

[*Note.* This bibliography is in no sense exhaustive. It intends to give the reader a selected list of publications which is representative both of the variety and complexity of the subject.]

Books

AMIDON, BEULAH. *Democracy's Challenge to Education.* New York: Farrar & Rinehart, 1940. 263 pp.
A symposium on the major issues of education, with contributions by W. A. Neilson, Ordway Tead, M. M. Stearns, and others.

BARZUN, JACQUES. *Of Human Freedom.* Boston: Little, Brown, 1939. 334 pp.
A philosophical defense of democracy which attacks all absolutistic belief as inimical to freedom.

BEESLEY, PATRICIA. *The Revival of the Humanities in American Education.* New York: Columbia University Press, 1940. 201 pp.
A survey of curricular programs which bear the title "humanities," together with an historical account of their development.

BODE, B. H. *Democracy as a Way of Life.* New York: The Macmillan Co., 1937. 114 pp.
Maintains that the school must train students to adapt their behavior to new conditions. The assumption of the argument is that schools at present are mainly training students for a society no longer existent.

———. *Progressive Education at the Crossroads.* New York: Newson, 1938. 128 pp.
Against a background of discussion of the ideals of progressive education and its development, the book offers a program for its reform, citing the need of greater emphasis on a social ideal, especially in professional education.

BOUCHER, C. S. *The Chicago College Plan.* Chicago: University of Chicago Press, 1935. 344 pp.
An exhaustive analysis and exposition of the curricular experiments at the University of Chicago.

CASWELL, H. L., AND CAMPBELL, D. S. *Readings in Curriculum Development.* New York: The American Book Co., 1937. 753 pp.
A selection of discussions of all phases of curricular problems and experiments which provides useful source material.

COKER, F. W. *Recent Political Thought.* New York: D. Appleton-Century Co., 1934. 574 pp.
Bibliography at the end of each chapter.
Discusses the controversy over the basic tenets of democracy as envisaged today and the problem of reconciling individual liberty to a successful functioning of government.

COLE, S. G. *Liberal Education in a Democracy.* New York: Harper & Brothers, 1940. 309 pp.
Against an historical background, the pattern of liberal education is examined in terms of six comprehensive areas of learning which constitute the core of a liberal education.

DEWEY, JOHN. *Democracy and Education.* New York. The Macmillan Co., 1916. 434 pp.
An examination of the function of education in democracy and of the interaction of democracy and education.

———. *Education Today.* Ed. by J. Ratner. New York: G. P. Putnam's Sons, 1940. 373 pp.
A collection of articles, the first of which was published in 1892, which gives a summary of Dewey's educational theories.

———. *Experience and Education.* New York: The Macmillan Co., 1938. 116 pp.
An examination of the controversy over progressive education and a defense of it by its founder.

———. *Freedom and Culture.* New York: G. P. Putnam's Sons, 1939. 176 pp.
A discussion of the nature of freedom and of those forces which shape and determine both its concept and its practice.

FLEXNER, A. *Universities: American, English, German.* New York: Oxford University Press, 1930. 381 pp.
Contrasting the methods and problems of English and German universities with those in America, Flexner points to the greater problems which mass education presents to American institutions.

GIDEONSE, H. D. *The Higher Learning in a Democracy.* New York: Farrar & Rinehart, 1937. 34 pp.
An attack on President Hutchins, especially his "The Higher Learning in America."

GRAY, W. S. (Editor) *General Education: Its Nature, Scope, and Essential Elements.* Chicago: University of Chicago Press, 1934. 188 pp.

An attempt to give a definition to the term "general education," and an examination of its content and aims. See especially the essay "The Relation of the Humanities to General Education," by H. M. Jones, pp. 39-52.

———. *Recent Trends in American College Education.* Chicago: University of Chicago Press, 1931. 253 pp.

An account of the growth of junior colleges and comprehensive examinations and tests.

GREENE, T. M. (Editor) *The Meaning of the Humanities.* Princeton: Princeton University Press, 1938. xxxix, 178 pp.

Essays by R. B. Perry, A. C. Krey, E. Panofsky, R. L. Calhoun, G. Chinard, and an introduction by T. M. Greene defining the concept of humanistic education.

HUTCHINS, R. M. *The Higher Learning in America.* New Haven: Yale University Press, 1936. 119 pp.

President Hutchins's attack on contemporary education and his defense of general education.

———. *No Friendly Voice.* Chicago: University of Chicago Press, 1936. 197 pp.

Collection of addresses on the educational function of a university in contemporary society.

JOHNSON, B. L. *What About Survey Courses?* New York: Henry Holt & Co., 1937. 377 pp.

A detailed survey of the content and administration of survey courses.

JOHNSON, J. B. *Education for Democracy. Essays and Addresses.* Minneapolis: University of Minnesota Press, 1934. 280 pp.

Collected essays and speeches of the author dealing with the problems of a liberal college, based on a belief in the progressive education movement.

———. *Scholarship and Democracy.* New York: D. Appleton-Century Co., 1937. 113 pp.

Raises the difficulty of providing adequate training for scholarship in mass education through a detailed study of student achievement in a college of liberal arts.

———. *The Liberal College in Changing Society.* New York: D. Appleton-Century Co., 1930. 326 pp.

Discusses the functions, objectives, and procedures of the liberal college. The relation of the college to the shaping of the intelligence needed by the management in democracy is the stated theme of the book.

KELLEY, R. L. *The American Colleges and the Social Order.* New York: The Macmillan Co., 1940. 380 pp.

The relationship of the college and the community is here examined in detail with emphasis laid on the necessity of adaptation of college training to contemporary social needs.

KILPATRICK, W. H. *Group Education for a Democracy.* New York: Association Press, 1940. 219 pp.

A collection of articles, formerly published, designed for those interested in the forces of education outside the school influencing adolescents.

———. *Remaking the Curriculum.* New York: Newson and Co., 1936. 128 pp.

Seven articles previously published in the Journal of the National Education Association, November, 1935—May, 1936, are included in this.

KNIGHT, E. W. *What College Presidents Say.* Chapel Hill: University of North Carolina Press, 1940. 337 pp.

States the purposes and weaknesses of higher education in an analysis of structural relationships of a college.

LYND, R. S. *Knowledge for What?* Princeton: Princeton University Press, 1939. 268 pp.

An examination of the role of social science in our culture and a plea for greater integration of social studies.

MEIKLEJOHN, A. *Education Between Two Worlds.* New York: Harper & Brothers, 1942. 303 pp.

A philosophical analysis of the predicament of liberal education at the present time.

NEVINS, ALLAN. *The Gateway to History.* New York: D. C. Heath, 1938. 412 pp.

An examination of theories of what constitutes "history" and a statement as to the effect of fluctuating theories on the interpretation of the past.

RUGG, H. *Culture and Education in America.* New York: Harcourt, Brace and Co., 1931. 404 pp.

A tentative outline of the chief concepts of American culture and of needed steps in educational reconstruction.

ULICH, ROBERT. *Fundamentals of Democratic Education: An Introduction to Educational Philosophy.* New York: American Book Co., 1940. 362 pp.

Discusses the role of education in relation to society, the state, and religion, while analyzing conflicting educational philosophies.

WHITEHEAD, A. N. *The Aims of Education and Other Essays*. New York: The Macmillan Co., 1929. 247 pp.
Reprinted in part from periodicals. The scientists' interpretation of the function of education in a world dominated by scientific and pseudo-scientific thought.

WRISTON, H. M. *The Nature of a Liberal College*. Appleton, Wis.: Lawrence College Press, 1937. 177 pp.
A statement of not only the aims of a liberal education but also of the role and value of a liberal college in contemporary society.

PERIODICALS

ADLER, M. J. "Education and Democracy." *Commonweal*, 29: 581-583. March 17, 1939.

———. "The Chicago School." *Harper's Magazine*, 183: 377-388. November, 1941.

———. "The Crisis in Contemporary Education." *Social Frontier*, 5: 140-145. February, 1939.

ANGELL, J. R. "Freedom for the University." *School and Society*, 43: 327-329. March 7, 1936.

———. "Scholar and the Specialist." *American Scholar*, 6, No. 3: 345-353. 1937.

———. "Some Possible Consequences of Advancing Standards in Schools and Colleges." *School and Society*, 43: 489-496. April 11, 1936.

ARBUTHNOT, C. C. "The Liberal Arts College and Vocational Education." *Association of American Colleges Bulletin*, XXV, 2: 299-304. May, 1939.

"Are the Humanities Doomed?" Editorial in *Association of American Colleges Bulletin*, X: 262-273. May, 1936.

ARLT, GUSTAVE, O. "The Humanities in a Scientific World." *Modern Language Forum*, XXIV, 3: 122. September, 1939.

BAGLEY, W. C. "Progressive Education is Too Soft." *Education*, 60: 75-81. October, 1939.

BARR, S. "Education of Freedom." *New Republic*, 107: 248-250. August 31, 1942.

BARZUN, J. "The Humanities: Proper Study of Mankind." *The English Journal*, College Edition, XXVII: 637-648. October, 1938.

BEARD, C. A. "Education Enriched by Living." *National Education Association Journal*, 7: 227-228. November, 1938.

BODE, B. H. "Education for Democracy." *School and Society*, 53: 152. February 1, 1941.

BOWMAN, I. "Graduate School in American Democracy." *United States Office Education Bulletin*, 10: 1-10. 1939.

BROWN, CARLETON. "The Attack on the Castle." *P. M. L. A.*, Supplement, LI: 1294-1306. 1936.

BUCHANAN, J. H. "Educators Responsibility in Our Democratic Society." *Phi Delta Kappa*. November, 1940.

BUTTS, R. F. "Liberal Education and the Prescribed Curriculum in the American College." *Educational Record*, XXVIII, 4: 548-564. October, 1937.

CARLSON, J. A. "The Biological Sciences." (Contribution to Liberal Education in the College.) *Association of American Colleges Bulletin*, XXIII, 1: 72-82. March, 1937.

CARMICHAEL, L. "Pragmatic Humanism and American Higher Education." *School and Society*, 48: 637-646. November 19, 1938.

CHIDSEY, H. "Culture in Education." *Journal of Higher Education*, VIII: 175-184. April, 1937.

CLARKE, E. T. "The Union of the Arts in the Liberal Arts College." *Association of American Colleges Bulletin*, XXIII, 3: 336-341. November, 1937.

CONANT, J. B. "Education for American Democracy: The Problem it Presents." *Vital Speeches*, 4: 418. May 1, 1938.

———. "Future of Our Higher Education." *Harper's Magazine*, 561-570. May, 1938.

———. "Liberal Education." *Vital Speeches*, 3: 253-256. February 1, 1937.

———. "The American College." *Association of American Colleges Bulletin*, XXIII, 1: 33-44. March, 1937.

CONKLIN, E. G. "Education for Demccracy." *School and Society*, 50: 161-170. August 5, 1939.

———. "The Place of Science in the Liberal Arts College." *Association of American Colleges Bulletin*, 487-498. December, 1938.

DAVIDSON, C. "The Liberal Arts of Maturity." *Association of American Colleges Bulletin*, XXV, 2: 213-220. May, 1939.

DAVIS, W. C. "Vocational and Liberal Education." *School and Society*, 55: 272-273. March 7, 1942.

"Democracy and Higher Education." Panel Discussion. *American Teacher*, 21-29. February, 1940.

DODDS, H. W. "College Level: Mental Laziness Masquerades as
Tolerance." *Vital Speeches*, 5: 30-32. October 15, 1938.
———. "Future of the Liberal Arts College." *Association of American
Colleges Bulletin*, XXIV, 2: 169-178. May, 1938.
———. "Objective of a Liberal Education." *Vital Speeches*, 17: 26-28.
October 15, 1940.
DOYLE, H. G. "Some Fundamental Problems for the Modern Lan-
guages and Literatures." *P.M.L.A.* Supplement, LIV: 1346-
1355. 1939.
DUCASSE, C. J. "Are the Humanities Worth Their Keep?" *The
American Scholar*, VI: 460-470. Autumn, 1937.
DYKSTRA, C. A. "Democracy and Education." *Vital Speeches*, 4: 527-
531. June 15, 1938.
EDMAN, I. "Man's Humanities to Man." *Saturday Review of Litera-
ture*, 20: 3-4. September 2, 1939.
EMBLER, W. B. "Toward a More Humane Education in the Hu-
manities." *Sewanee Review*, 48: 51-65. January, 1940.
FREEMAN, S. A. "Humanities to the Defense of Democracy." *Educa-
tion*, 62: 372-382. February, 1942.
GLASS, META. "The Contribution of the Humanities." *Bulletin of
the Association of American Colleges*, XXIII: 55-63. March,
1937.
GREENE, T. M. and others. "The Unity of a Liberal Arts Education."
Association of American Colleges Bulletin, 218-225. May, 1941.
GREY, LENNOX. "The English Teacher Faces the Humanities."
Teacher's College Record, XXXIX: 31-50. October, 1937.
GROSS, A. A. "What is Involved in Being Educated?" *Journal of
Adult Education*, XI, 4: 376-380. October, 1939.
HARRIS, R. C. "University Education in the Crisis of Democracy."
Association of American Colleges Bulletin, XXIV, 2: 187-200.
May, 1938.
HAVENS, P. S. "How Can We Keep the Humanities Humane?" Pro-
ceedings of the Fifty-first Annual Convention of the Middle
States Association of Colleges and Secondary Schools, 70-74,
1937. Published by the Association, 1938.
HOLLINSHEAD, B. S. "The Relations Between the Liberal Arts College,
the Junior College and the Professional School." *Association
of American Colleges Bulletin*, XXVI, 1: 64-72. March, 1940.
HOLMES, H. N. "The Physical Sciences" (Contribution to Liberal
Education in Colleges). *Association of American Colleges Bulletin*, XXIII, 1: 67-72. March, 1937.

HOPKINS, E. M. "The Role of the Liberal Arts College in American Higher Education." *Association of American Colleges Bulletin,* XXIII, 14: 437-439. December, 1937.

HUTCHINS, J. M. "Democracy and Education." *Vital Speeches,* 5: 586-588. July 15, 1939.

———. "Tradition in Education." *Vital Speeches,* 4: 258-262. February 15, 1938.

———. "Education for Freedom." *Harper's Magazine.* 183: 512-526. October, 1941.

JACKS, L. P. "Why Greek and Latin?" *Spectator* (London), 163: 500-501. October 13, 1939.

JERNEGAN, M. W. "Productivity of Doctors of Philosophy in History." *Association of American Colleges Bulletin,* XII: 184-196. April, 1927.

JONES, E. S. "Comprehensive Examinations in the Humanities." *Association of American Colleges Bulletin,* XXIII, 2: 207-318. May, 1938. (See pp. 211-216.)

JONES, H. M. "The American Scholar Once More." *Harvard Alumni Bulletin,* XXXIX: 732-739. March 26, 1937.

———. "The General Educational Stream of the Liberal Arts." *Harvard Alumni Bulletin,* 1019-1025. June 3, 1938.

———. "The Relation of the Humanities to General Education." General Education (Proceedings of the Institute for Administrative Officers of Higher Education), VII: 39-58. 1934.

KANDEL, I. L. "The Fantasia of Current Education." *The American Scholar,* 10: 286-297. Summer, 1941.

———. "The Meaning of a Liberal Education." *Teachers College Record,* 91-101. November, 1939.

KILPATRICK, W. H. "Propaganda, Democracy and Education." *School and Society,* 49: 405-409. April 1, 1939.

KLEIN, A. "Survey of Land Grant Colleges and Universities." U. S. Department of the Interior, *Office of Education Bulletin,* II: 9. Washington, D. C., U. S. Government Printing Office, 1930.

KNIGHTS, L. C. "University Teaching of English and History: A Plea for Correlation." *Southern Review,* 5, 3: 511-523. Winter, 1940.

LELAND, W. G. "Recent Trends in the Humanities." *Science,* N. S. LXXIX: 281-285. March 30, 1934.

LIPPMANN, W. "Education Without Culture." *Commonweal,* 33: 322-325. January 17, 1941.

LOWELL, A. L. "Democracy, Equality and Education." *Harvard Teachers Record,* 1: 94-98. November, 1931.

LOWRY, H. F. "The Old and the New Humanities." *Classical Journal,* XXXVI: 197-210. January, 1941.

MACLEISH, A. "Education in Uniform: The Dilemma." *Atlantic Monthly.* 171: 37-40. February, 1943.

McKEON, R. "The Humanities and Humanisms." *The University of Chicago Magazine,* 25: 10-11. December, 1939.

MANLY, J. M. "Humanistic Studies and Science." *Speculum.* V, 3: 243-250. July, 1930.

MEIKLEJOHN, A. "Future of Liberal Education." *New Republic,* 108: 113-115. January 25, 1943.

MIMS, E. "The Humanities—Past and Present." *Association of American Colleges Bulletin,* XXV, 4: 505-514. December, 1939.

Modern Language Association. Committee of Twenty-Four. "The Aims of the Teaching of Literature." *Journal of Higher Education,* X: 330-333. June, 1939.

MOULTON, H. G. "The Social Sciences." (Contributions to Liberal Education in the Colleges.) *Association of American Colleges Bulletin,* XXIII, 1: 82-90. March, 1937.

NASON, J. W. "Nature and Content of a Liberal Education." *Association of American Colleges Bulletin,* XXVII, 1: 53-61. March, 1941.

ORTON, D. "Liberal Education and the Modern World." *Journal of Higher Education,* 237-242. May, 1939.

PROKOSCH, E. "Treason Within the Castle." *P. M. L. A. Supplement,* LII: 1320-1329. 1937.

PULLIAS, E. V. "Liberal Education's Greatest Need: Teachers." *School and Society,* 56: 436-438. November 7, 1942.

SCHÜTZE, M. "Toward a Modern Humanism." *P. M. L. A.,* II: 284-299. March, 1936.

STUDEBAKER, J. W. "Education for Democracy." *School and Society,* 43: 305-311. March 7, 1936.

———. "Education Moves Democracy Forward." *Vital Speeches,* 5: 726-729. September 15, 1939.

TEAD, ORDWAY. "Charter for a College." *Association of American Colleges Bulletin,* XXV: 393-407. 1939.

TOLLEY, W. P. "Higher Education and Good Government." *Association of American Colleges Bulletin,* XXIV, 2: 209-217. May, 1938.

ULICH, R. "Some Ultimate Values." *Harvard Educational Review*, 406-428. October, 1940.

UPHAM, A. H. "Liberal Arts Ride the Wave." *School and Society*, 55: 113-117. January 31, 1942.

WILSON, H. E. "Democracy and Education." *Harvard Educational Review*, 390-393. October, 1939.

WRIGHT, L. B. "The Retreat of the Humanities." *The English Journal*, College Edition, XXVIII, 2: 121-132. February, 1939.

WRISTON, H. M. "Education for the Defense of Democracy." *Proceedings of the Academy of Political Science*, 288-299. May, 1939.

———. "General Education in Liberal Arts Colleges." *Harvard Educational Review*, 279-286. May 19, 1939.

———. "Liberal Learning." *Association of American Colleges Bulletin*, XXV, 3: 365-369. November, 1939.

ZINSSER, H. "What is a Liberal Education?" *School and Society*, 45: 801-807. June 12, 1937.

REPORTS

AMERICAN AND CANADIAN COMMITTEES ON MODERN LANGUAGES. Coleman, Algernon. *The Teaching of Modern Foreign Languages in the United States*. Vol. 12. New York: The Macmillan Co., 1931. 299 pp.
A synthesis of all the findings of the Committee on Investigation of the Modern Foreign Language Study. The report is exhaustive within the range of its investigation, that is, the secondary school and the corresponding courses in modern language in college.

AMERICAN ASSOCIATION OF SCHOOL ADMINISTRATORS. Graves, E. P. *American Education and Democracy*. Official Report. 1941. pp. 91-93.

AMERICAN ASSOCIATION OF UNIVERSITY PROFESSORS. *Depression, Recovery and Higher Education*. New York: McGraw-Hill Book Co., 1937, 543 pp.
A report by Committees of the American Association of University Professors.

AMERICAN CLASSICAL LEAGUE.
The Classical Investigation. Part 1. General Report. A Summary of Results with Recommendations for the Organization of the Course in Secondary Latin and for the Improvement in

Methods of Teaching. American Classical League, 1934. Abridged Edition, 235 pp.

The findings of a three-year investigation which included collaboration of scholars in England and France with the avowed purpose of improving the teaching of the classics.

AMERICAN COUNCIL ON EDUCATION. *What the High Schools Ought to Teach.* Report of Special Committee for the American Youth Commission. Washington, D. C., 1940. 36 pp.

Prescott, D. A. *Emotion and the Educative Process.* A Report of the Commission on the Relation of Emotion to the Educative Process. Washington, D. C., 1938. 323 pp.

The findings of a four-year investigation of the relationship between the emotional condition of a child and his ability as a student.

AMERICAN HISTORICAL ASSOCIATION.

Bagley, W. C., and Alexander, T. *The Teacher of the Social Studies.* Report of the Commission on the Social Studies. Part XIV. New York: Charles Scribner's Sons, 1937. 328 pp.

Deals with the professional aspects of the selection and training of teachers for the social sciences in the schools.

Beard, C. A. *A Charter for the Social Sciences.* Report of the Commission on the Social Studies. Part 1. New York: Charles Scribner's Sons, 1932. 121 pp.

Statement of the founding of the Commission. The introductory volume to the reports of the Commission.

Beard, C. A. *The Nature of the Social Sciences.* Report of the Commission on the Social Studies. Part VII. New York: Charles Scribner's Sons, 1934. 236 pp.

A statement of the nature and meaning of the social sciences designed to serve as a background for the consideration of the objectives in education.

Conclusions and Recommendations of the Commission. Report of the Commission on the Social Studies. New York: Charles Scribner's Sons, 1943. 169 pp.

Counts, G. S. *The Social Foundations of Education.* Report of the Commission on the Social Studies, Part IX. New York: Charles Scribner's Sons, 1934. 579 pp.

An examination of the development of American society from the time of its definite organization to the present, in which the school is considered as an instrument of society.

Horn, Ernest. *Methods of Instruction in the Social Studies.* American Historical Association. Report of the Commission on the Social Studies. Part XV. New York: Charles Scribner's Sons, 1937. 523 pp.

The dissenting opinion to the conclusions and recommendations of the Commission.

The Study of History in the Schools. The Report of the Committee of Five. Annual Report of American Historical Association for 1910. Washington, 1912. pp. 209-242.

A report historically important because of its effect on the teaching of history, which used the earlier report of the Committee of Seven as starting point, but which was the result of an entirely new survey and interpretation.

The Study of History in the Schools. Report of the Committee of Seven. Annual Report of the American Historical Association for 1898. Washington, 1899. pp. 427-564.

This report exerted great influence on the teaching of history and the history curricula in the United States.

Tryon, R. M. *The Social Sciences as School Subjects.* Report of the Commission on the Social Studies. New York: Charles Scribner's Sons, 1935. 541 pp.

A detailed discussion of what has been and is studied in the realm of social sciences as school subjects.

CARNEGIE FOUNDATION.

Eells, W. C. *Surveys of American Higher Education.* New York, 1937. 538 pp.

A study of all surveys of higher education, which appraises their value.

CARNEGIE FOUNDATION FOR THE ADVANCEMENT OF TEACHING.

The College and the Freshman. Study of the Relations of Secondary and Higher Education in Pennsylvania. Progress Report II. Carnegie Foundation for the Advancement of Teaching, New York, 1930. 48 pp.

Learned, W. S., and Wood, B. D. *The Student and his Knowledge.* Bulletin No. 29, New York, 1938. 406 pp.

The report to the Carnegie Foundation of the results of the examinations of 1928, 1930, and 1932 given in the Pennsylvania Survey. The most ambitious and authoritative survey of this type.

CONGRESS ON EDUCATION FOR DEMOCRACY.
Education for Democracy. The proceedings of the Congress. The Bureau of Publications, Teachers College, Columbia, New York, 1939. 466 pp.
Addresses by both English and American leaders on what constitutes training for life in a democracy.

INSTITUTE FOR ADMINISTRATIVE OFFICERS OF HIGHER INSTITUTIONS. Gray, W. S. (Editor) *Recent Trends in American College Education.* Vol. IV. Chicago: University of Chicago Press, 1931. 353 pp.

MODERN LANGUAGE ASSOCIATION.
Fries, C. C. *Language Study in American Education.* With the co-operation of W. M. Sale and E. H. Zeydel. Commission on Trends in Education of the Modern Language Association. New York, 1940. 40 pp.

H. M. Jones, Chairman. *Modern Language Association Report.* (Mimeographed) Report of the Committee on Educational Trends adverse to the teaching of the modern languages and literatures.

NATIONAL COUNCIL OF THE TEACHERS OF ENGLISH. Report of the Committee on Correlation. New York. D. Appleton-Century Co., 1936.
An investigation of the correlated curriculum.

NATIONAL EDUCATION ASSOCIATION.
The Improvement of Education: its interpretation for democracy. Fifteenth Yearbook. Washington: The Association, 1937. 328 pp.
The need of interpreting the aims of education to the public.

Educational Policies Commission. Beard, C. A. *The Unique Function of Education in American Democracy.* Washington: The Association, 1937. 129 pp.
An historical summary of the function of education in our democracy from its founding.

Educational Policies Commission. *Education and Economic Wellbeing in American Democracy.* Washington: The Association, 1940. 217 pp.
The kinds of education for economic well-being put against a statement of the economic challenge to an American ideal.

Educational Policies Commission. *The Purpose of Education in American Democracy.* Washington: The Association, 1938. 157 pp.

The chief objectives of the educational process are treated separately, together with an analysis of the democratic process.

Educational Policies Commission. *The Structure and Administration of Education in American Democracy*. Washington: The Association, 1938. 116 pp.

Discusses the administration of local, state, and federal school administrative programs.

NATIONAL SOCIETY FOR THE STUDY OF EDUCATION. *Changes and Experiments in Liberal Education*. 31st Yearbook. Part II. 1932.

General Education in the Liberal Arts College. 38th Yearbook. Part II. Bloomington, Ill., 1939.

Wriston, H. M. *A Critical Appraisal of Experiments in General Education*. 38th Yearbook. Part II. Bloomington, Ill., 1939. pp. 297-321.

An attack on general education, experimentation, and progressive education.

THE ADVISORY COMMITTEE ON EDUCATION.

Reeves, F. W. (Chairman) Report of the Committee. Washington: U.S. Government Printing Office, 1938. 243 pp.

The report of the committee appointed by President Roosevelt, September 19, 1936, to investigate the need of federal aid to education, especially to vocational training.

THE JOHN DEWEY SOCIETY.

Rugg, H. (Editor) *Democracy and the Curriculum*. Third Yearbook. D. Appleton-Century Company, 1939. 536 pp.

Purports to be a guide for teachers, youth, and their parents in the study of the American Problem.

THE REGENT'S INQUIRY.

Spaulding, F. T. *High School and Life*. New York: McGraw-Hill Book Co., 1938. 377 pp.

Discusses especially preparation for citizenship and vocation by the schools of New York. Conclusion is that they are failing.